Beyond Belief:
Stories of a Newly Qualified Paramedic

Georgia Combes

About The Author

Georgia Combes has been a registered paramedic with the HCPC since 2019, spending the first two years of her practice under the title 'Newly Qualified Paramedic' (NQP), immediately after completing a three year BSc degree in Paramedic Science. NQPs are expected to demonstrate active consolidation for 24 months whilst under the support of senior colleagues, before they are deemed experienced enough to practice without the need for additional guidance.

In this honest memoir, Georgia describes how caring for her disabled mother from the age of 14, initially drove her to become a paramedic despite mental health and an unsupportive family. Before sharing brutally frank, chronological, reflective accounts of her time as an NQP, facing grief, heartbreak, doubt, fear, dread, wonder, overwhelming joy, surprise, desperation, but never boredom! On numerous occasions, for the first time. This is her first book.

Copyright © 2024 by Georgia Combes

All rights reserved

No portion of this book may be reproduced in any form without written permission from the publisher or author, except as permitted by UK copyright law.

Preface:

The most common question I am asked is 'what's the worst job you've ever seen?' The truth is, it's not what people think. I am expected to regale some horrific, traumatic, major incident, leaving the ambulance and my freshly washed uniform covered head to toe in blood, vomit and cerebral matter!

But the worst jobs aren't these at all. They are actually those that leave an empty, wrenching feeling in the pit of your stomach, that tie you up in knots, sometimes for hours, sometimes for days. Those that make you feel something no human should ever feel. Those that make words come out your mouth you never expected to leave your lips. The feeling you get after you see a twenty year old hanging from a basketball hoop, or the sounds that somehow form the words from your tongue that tell a child they're never going to see their deceased Mother ever again.

The fact that I'm still asked this same question over and over again, regularly makes me realise what a unique -and privileged- position paramedics are in, to see both the worst and the best of human life - and death. But it also makes me realise that what my colleagues and I witness routinely, is not something the unexposed general public can even begin to imagine. How could they; if they insist on brutally interrogating me with that question?

This prompted the 'Beyond Belief: True Stories of a Newly Qualified Paramedic', to give the public just a small insight into what being a paramedic is really about, whether you may wish to pursue this as a dream yourself, or you're generally curious. Why paramedics lie when we tell you what the worst job we've ever seen is. Why we regale some traumatic car crash of a scene like we're blood thirsty monsters, instead of the truth. Because the truth is, when you ask us that question, you don't really want the real answer. Not in that moment, when your excited, gleaming eyes look in anticipation awaiting the answer, in the middle of the busy high street or in front of your children. But whilst you sit down and open the pages to this book, if you really want the truth, the real truth? Here it is...

In order to maintain confidentiality and respect, and abide by my professional standards of proficiency and conduct, names, dates and times have not been disclosed, whilst places and locations have been altered.

Prologue:

I remember when I first wanted to be a paramedic, I was blinded by the illusion of *Casualty* and *Holby City*, which I would watch every Saturday night with my disabled Mum, in awe, from the age of thirteen or fourteen. But it wasn't until a real ambulance was called out for my Mum with brain damage, I really made the conscious decision that I too would become a paramedic for the rest of my working life. They were like gods working there in front of me. I was a love struck teenager, but not for a boy, -or a girl- for a career, a life choice. I told my Mum of my future plans on the way out of a GP appointment I had taken her to one day. She didn't take me seriously at first, but why on earth would she? My career plans changed every five minutes at that age, from a chef to an artist to a fashion designer to a carpenter! But this one stuck.

No one thought I could do it though, not my teachers, not my Nan and certainly not my Mum. But I thank them. I used that lack of faith and their negative assumptions as fuel. The more I was told I would never achieve my dream, the more determined I became.

I became almost obsessed with the idea. Nowadays I have no idea why I was so obsessed, when I am called to put a plaster on a stubbed toe! But I suppose there are much worse things for a teenage girl to obsess about. I would get home from school and memorise all two hundred and six bones in the body, then the hormones. I had so many of my own flying around at that age it made sense to learn them. Then the muscles; the muscles were a lot harder. I can still name all the bones in the human body today from when I used to sit in my room for hours on end as a spotty teenager, thinking I knew everything there was to know about the world.

I left school with nine GCSEs, but my teachers laughing at me at the thought of me becoming a paramedic, one in particular. She was the kind that tells all her students- apart from her one or two favourites- they'll amount to nothing in life and there's no point in even trying.

I don't know why they had such little faith in me. Maybe because they thought I couldn't hold my own as I was bullied through primary and secondary school quite extensively and acquired anxiety as a result, since before I can remember. If only kids – and some teachers alike- knew the consequences of their actions. I was also extremely shy in school, I would cry an awful lot and appeared to only develop proper social skills later in my adult life. I left with zero confidence and no idea how to live in this world -maybe that was why my teachers laughed at me of the thought of me becoming a paramedic- but I had a goal, and nothing was going to stop me.

At eighteen things were looking up. I got my diploma, but was just short of a few university and college admission points (UCAS) to get into my chosen university, so I booked myself onto a medical science diploma for a year. Unfortunately though, my mental health declined and subsequently when I applied for the paramedic degree, I failed to get a place on the course. I went into a reckless manic depressive state. If I wasn't going to be a paramedic then what was I? I had no plan B, no master backup plan, so I did what I thought all eighteen year olds with no life goals did, I conformed to the stereotype. I lived a life of no consequences, partying all night three or four times a week, consuming large quantities of alcohol, buying spontaneous tattoo's, pets and expensive items I had no idea what to do with; I felt invincible. I lost two stone in weight and was paranoid all the time; I confirmed everybody's expectations, I was never going to be a paramedic, and that killed me.

This followed with a deep depression that seemed to last a lifetime. I was tested for Bipolar, but the truth is, I wasn't manic depressive, I was just a heartbroken troubled teenager who needed to grow the hell up!

I can't pinpoint a day, or a time in my life when I came out of this hell hole, but I do remember as a teaching assistant in a special educational needs (SEN) school, I began feeling hope again. It was now five years since I had applied for university and I hadn't mentioned being a paramedic once, but all of a sudden, it began consuming me once more. Why couldn't I be a paramedic? I was a totally different person to the one I was five years prior. I made myself list all the reasons I shouldn't just try, and I couldn't think of any. I still had so many doubts though, what if this was just a childhood dream made up by fictitious TV shows? What if my Mum was right all along, she knows me best, right? I must remember she has brain damage. I applied to go back to college anyway, despite my fears.

***

The 16th January that year was a bitter-sweet day. It was the worst day of my life, but the day my Mum and I both knew I was undoubtedly going to be a paramedic. My seventy four year old Nan, who we were all extremely close to, was due to visit that morning after her routine GP appointment. She was extremely fit and healthy with no co-morbidities, so nobody worried when she didn't initially show up at the expected time and wasn't answering her phone. She probably got held up at the GP or was doing a spot of shopping before she arrived, which she'd often do. Besides, she never had her phone switched on! She'd only ever turn it on to send a text, before immediately switching it off again without even looking to see if she'd got a reply. By 12:30 though –two hours after she was due- I started window twitching and became increasingly concerned. I kept suggesting:

"Maybe I should just cycle round to her bungalow, just to check everything's ok?"

I had dreamt the night before that she'd passed away and I woke up that morning so relieved it was just a dream, but what were the chances of that actually being a premonition? Mum kept saying: "We'll go together in ten minutes" every ten minutes.

She didn't want to even contemplate what we might find, and I can't blame her. Eventually, we agreed to get in a taxi and head to my Nan's bungalow at 14:15, when the afternoon drama Doctors finished. It's funny, I can't stand any medical TV show now, especially fictitious ones! I don't remember a single thing of that episode, I was counting down the minutes and seconds until 14:15, praying her car would just pull into our driveway before we left, and we'd all laugh for being so anxious. But she didn't. When we arrived in a taxi at my beloved Nan's home, we expected to find her on the floor following a fall with a NOF* fracture or something similar, but what we actually found was far, far worse. All the curtains were shut, so we let ourselves in with the spare key.

"Nan?" "Mum?" We shouted. No response.

After scanning her living room, I opened her bedroom door, and there she was. She was in her pyjamas, laid supine next to her un-slept bed, with a full cup of now cold cocoa on her bedside table. Her face and chest were covered in very dark red dried blood, almost the same colour as the cocoa. It appeared to have come from her ears, nose and mouth. She had also been incontinent, which made me think she'd had a seizure before she stopped breathing.

After taking it all in for a second, I exited the bedroom and quickly closed the door behind me for mum not to see the disturbing scene.

"Sit down Mum, we need to ring an ambulance" I said calmly.

"Is she in there? Where is she Georgia?"

"Sit down" I tell her again, firmly this time "There's something I need to tell you".   She quickly brushes past me before I can stop her and rushes into the bedroom frantically; as quickly as you can with two walking sticks. She screams, that heart wrenching painful scream I'd never heard before. She was –understandably- uncontrollably hysterical.

"My Mum" she sobbed "That's… my Mum" unable to string a sentence together through the tears. I hold her for what seems like hours, but in reality it's only really a few seconds, before I help carry her to the living room and make her a hot drink.

"I'm going to ring an ambulance" I tell her, reassuring her I won't be long.

Nan had been gone a long time, verging on twenty four hours we expect. She was ice cold and in rigor mortis. Mum even thought the dried blood on her face was spilt cocoa it was that dark now. I felt like the call handler just wasn't listening to me when I told her this information though.

"Right, I want you to put both hands on her chest and count with me: One… Two…Three…"

"No she's not workable, she's as stiff as a board and ice cold" I interrupt.

"Even so, count with me: One...Two...Three..." the call handler repeated.

I tried hard not to get annoyed; I couldn't have my Mum thinking I wasn't in control of the situation, so I reluctantly remained calm. Thankfully, just then, the ambulance crew came rushing through the front door, all their heavy resuscitation kit in tow, and I led them to the bedroom. I was in awe of them, again. Funnily enough, I know both of those clinician's well now. As soon as they saw her one shakes his head and the rush subsides. They enter the living room and do their usual amazing job of comforting Mum. I too stay strong for my Mum. It's only later that night alone do I grieve.

It turned out as we had expected, she'd had a massive subarachnoid brain haemorrhage*. She left a massive void in all our lives, but in some respect it gave us the kick up the ass we all needed. My youngest sister got into university to study Law, my Mum bought a house three hours away for a fresh start, and I got my shit together. I got my driving licence, climbed Kilimanjaro for charity -it was here I found my love for the outdoors and climbing- moved out, and above all, got into university to study paramedic science. That hot summers day when I found out I was going to university to train to be a paramedic was without a doubt the happiest day of my life, and the second time that year I had cried hard, but that time out of pure elation. I loved university and placement just as much as I had imagined, if not more, and I grew up so quickly studying and working on the front line. I had to. I was finally the confident, semi-intelligent person I longed to become all those years prior. Moreover, I met the love of my life 'A'. He's a paramedic and has been for ten years. He filled in for two weeks whilst my mentor was on his honeymoon. In that two weeks I found he shared my love for climbing and the outdoors, he was passionate about his work, funny and undoubtedly handsome. I fell in love with him immediately.

Now here I am, a newly qualified paramedic (NQP), with my own professional registration and the happiest, yet the most terrified I've ever been.

Contents

Preface: 5
Prologue: 7
CHAPTER ONE: 19
CHAPTER TWO: 25
CHAPTER THREE: 28
CHAPTER FOUR: 39
CHAPTER FIVE: 44
CHAPTER SIX: 48
CHAPTER SEVEN: 56
CHAPTER EIGHT: 61
CHAPTER NINE: 65
CHAPTER TEN: 70
CHAPTER ELEVEN: 76
CHAPTER TWELVE: 81
CHAPTER THIRTEEN: 86
CHAPTER FOURTEEN: 90
CHAPTER FIFTEEN: 92
CHAPTER SIXTEEN: 95
CHAPTER SEVENTEEN: 101
CHAPTER EIGHTEEN: 103
CHAPTER NINTEEN: 106
CHAPTER TWENTY: 110
CHAPTER TWENTY ONE: 113

CHAPTER TWENTY TWO: 118
CHAPTER TWENTY THREE: 125
CHAPTER TWENTY FOUR: 131
CHAPTER TWENTY FIVE: 136
CHAPTER TWENTY SIX: 141
CHAPTER TWENTY SEVEN: 146
CHAPTER TWENTY EIGHT:.............................151
CHAPTER TWENTY NINE: 155
CHAPTER THIRTY: 164
CHAPTER THIRTY ONE: 168
CHAPTER THIRTY TWO: 172
CHAPTER THIRTY THREE: 176
CHAPTER THIRTY FOUR: 180
CHAPTER THIRTY FIVE:...................................185
CHAPTER THIRTY SIX: 189
CHAPTER THIRTY SEVEN:...............................194
CHAPTER THIRTY EIGHT:................................200
CHAPTER THIRTY NINE: 203
CHAPTER FOURTY: 208
CHAPTER FOURTY ONE:..................................214
CHAPTER FOURTY TWO: 219
CHAPTER FOURTY THREE: 225
CHAPTER FOURTY FOUR:................................233
CHAPTER FOURTY FIVE:..................................238

CHAPTER FOURTY SIX:....................................251
Glossary (in order of sequence): 262
Acknowledgements 277

CHAPTER ONE:

Preceptorship

As I'm fresh faced from university I'm currently undergoing a preceptorship week, which in the ambulance service simply means I'm working as a double paramedic crew for my first three shifts, as opposed to the normal emergency care assistant (ECA) and paramedic crews. My first day at the beginning of the week I was absolutely bricking it. It was the day I had been waiting for and fascinating about since I was fourteen, but there I was, filled with utter terror that patients' lives were quite literally in my hands. I felt like a fraud, like someone just handed me their registration to play with for the day. How could this be mine? Had I done enough to earn it? Would I lose it in a mere few days? All questions that hadn't occurred to me until I was sat in the drivers' seat of an ambulance. With a couple of shifts under my belt now though, I think I'm starting to find my feet. It's just like being a year three student again, but without my mentor stood over my shoulder watching my every move. My safety netting. So not really the same at all. I reiterate on station a few times to my colleagues:

"I just feel like I'm winging it", only to be met with "I'm still winging it and I've been doing it ten years now".

I laugh, but I know this isn't strictly true. Paramedics are well trained clinicians'. Maybe I'm just letting my doubts get the better of me?

Today the paramedic I'm working with forgot to renew her registration, so is seen by the Trust as nothing more than an ECA, although she is of course a highly trained professional. Therefore, neither of us are permitted to work alone, so management take another paramedic who's working on the rapid response vehicle (RRV) off the car, and put him with us, making us a three manned paramedic crew.

We're getting on great. We're splitting the driving and attending between the three of us nicely, so when a cardiac arrest comes through, I'm excited at the prospect of us working together as a team. As we rush up the patient's stairs- why are these jobs always on the top floor(?)- we are met by a grieving wife and a body that looks like it's been completely still, in the same position for hours. There's no mistaking a corpse for somebody sleeping, they're very distinct, almost like a wax work, even when recently deceased. None of us expect this gentleman to be workable just by looking at him, so our sense of urgency subsides. He is slumped back on his kitchen floor, white as a sheet, eyes wide in a fixed gaze. His clothes are stained in food and urine, and are hanging off of him, as if they were lent to him by an obese friend. One of my colleagues takes the Wife into the other room to comfort her and gather a history, while we put the defibrillation pads on the patient to confirm our suspicions, as per protocol.

We can't believe it, he's in pulseless electrical activity (PEA). There are four cardiac arrest rhythms: Ventricular fibrillation (VF), ventricular tachycardia (VT), asystole, and PEA. In Pulseless VT and VF the heart is still in motion, but not in a way which is compatible with life. Therefore the patient has no pulse and no breathing pattern. These rhythms can be shocked with a defibrillator, which stops the heart altogether then restarts it. Similar to a computer crashing, often turning it off and on again does the trick. Asystole is what most people think of as death; a solid flat line with a single continuous beep indicating no signs of life whatsoever, the heart itself is completely motionless. This is what VT, VF and PEA will quickly progress to if not reversed. In asytole, if there is no rigor mortis, or other signs incompatible with life (decapitation, incineration etc.) and bystander CPR has been in progress, then we continue resuscitation attempts for twenty minutes only. Finally, in PEA the electrical impulses which create a heartbeat are fully intact, yet for some reason the heart muscle isn't pumping. This is often due to a defect to the pump, or no blood left in the circulatory system to pump around the body.

I quickly get on the chest whilst I shout for our colleague to return, and we commence a full resuscitation in this couples quaint but compact kitchen. One of us takes the airway, securing an endotracheal (ET) tube* into the patient's trachea, before forcing oxygen directly into their lungs, whilst my colleague takes over chest compressions and I look for a vein to cannulate, to administer drugs. There's nothing in his arms, but there's a whopper in his neck. It's his jugular.

"I've never cannulated a jugular before" I confide in my crew mates.

"Go for it!" One of them shouts out.

I'm nervous, but I remember this patient is deceased, I cannot make his condition any worse. As the positive outcome far outweighs the risk, I go for it. I see the tip of the cannula disappear horizontally into his neck as I pierce the skin. No flashback*. I advance the needle, still no flashback. I hope by some miracle that on slowly withdrawing the needle I'll hit a vein, but I don't. Damn! I missed. There's no blood even leaving the exit point of the needle as I failed to penetrate a single blood vessel, I didn't go deep enough.
"Here let me have a go" one of the other paramedics suggests confidently, whilst I take over the airway. Another crew have arrived at this point. Just as I start my handover for them I notice my knee suddenly getting wet and my colleague F'ing and blinding under his breath. There is blood pooling around the patient's neck and head. He pushed the cannula too deep and burst the vein; the CPR must be good as the blood is weeping out now. It only stops when we perform a rhythm check*.

"For fuck sake" the paramedic responsible snaps.

"That's why I don't cannulate jugulars" another paramedic laughs. I'm just as mortified, I didn't get it in either, but we both know now is no time to be feeling sorry for ourselves, we need to get on with the job in hand. It's clear none of us are going to get a cannula in this patient on taking another look at his arms, so we administer drugs intraosseously (IO)* straight into his tibia. Forty minutes later we're alternating chest compressions, -to prevent compression fatigue - life saving medications are being pumped around the patient's body, and he's receiving more than enough oxygen directly into his lungs to keep his brain oxygenated. Additionally, the bleeding from his neck has now subsided, and only turned out to be minimal in the end anyway after pressure and gauze was applied. Unfortunately though we're just not getting him back. His PEA rate is now less than ten beats per minute and has been for well over twenty minutes, so we make the team decision to call it. Time of Death 18:30 exactly. Half an hour past our finish time, but none of us care, we are all just disappointed we can't save him this time. This is unfortunately the harsh reality. On average only 5% of out of hospital cardiac arrests survive. We await the police who act on behalf of the coroner and regret to inform the wife. She explains he has been feeling generally unwell for weeks, but refused to see a doctor, and the last few days he has been unable to get out of bed due to feeling so weak. When he has been awake for only two to three hours a day, he has been delirious. Even in his final moments whilst in and out of consciousness, following collapsing on the kitchen floor when he tried to walk to make himself a drink, he still made his wife promise him not to phone for an ambulance. It was only when she couldn't wake him and realised he had stopped breathing she dialled 999. I can't understand why the elder generation feel like asking for help is bothering us, but sadly it's something we come across daily in the ambulance service. The elderly falling in the night, waiting until the morning to ask for help as they 'don't want to bother anybody'. Or the ultimate tragedy, them begging their spouses' to not bother anyone, causing them to die due to a lack of treatment. It's a generation thing, and the only reason behind it I can possibly think of is these strong men and woman fought for our country back in the day, and they survived without asking for anyone's help then, so why ask for it now? It was survival of the fittest and that stubborn but heroic nature never leaves them.

CHAPTER TWO:

Politics

It's been almost two weeks since my registration came through, which authorises me to practice as a paramedic, and I'm already having to work really hard not to get involved in the politics. I know every job has the playground camaraderie that is all too common in modern day society, and that it's almost impossible to avoid, but I've met a handful of clinicians now who have somehow managed to remain uninfluenced by the negativity, and I aspire to be one of them. They demonstrate an utter disinterest in the monotonous remarks, groans, sarcastic comments and damn right drama, but unfortunately they come very few and far between in this -and every other- overworked industry. Don't get me wrong, I completely understand the bitterness and utter despair with pressure from the Control room to finish each and every job as quickly as possible, to avoid a welfare check - Controls way of asking you why you're taking so long when there are another thirty calls stacking, and no ambulances to attend any of them. and pressure to finish on time. Then there's the pressure of being with a patient who has taken six paracetamol in an attempt to end their life, but they are refusing to attend the emergency department (ED) and claim as soon as you leave the scene, they'll take more pills; but they have full mental capacity so you can't drag them out of their homes, that would be classed as kidnapping. And although you agree ED is not the most suitable place for them, it is the only 'safe place' available to ambulance crews at 2 o clock in the morning. So you desperately attempt to convince them that ED will have a psychiatrist who can help them, which it does, but they'll likely be waiting in a crowded waiting room for six hours to see them. Then in addition to all this, when you arrive at ED which has already reached full capacity with occupied beds queuing out into the corridors, backed up onto the offloading ambulances outside, you have to justify to the nurse in charge why your patient deserves a bed.

Finally when the sun comes up and you think your night shift is coming to an end eleven and a half hours in, control have an outstanding category one (cat 1)* call- the highest priority call out which presents an immediate threat to life. And as you are the only resource available, you attend, making your twelve hour shift a now fourteen hour shift. That gives you just over ten hours to drive home, sleep, eat and drive back to work thirty minutes early for your next shift that evening, where you'll do it all over again. And just when you think you are doing a good job and making a positive difference to society, you open your emails to find you haven't been meeting the average expected on scene times and have had your annual leave for your birthday refused. Again.

Fortunately, for me the rewards and utter privilege of being a paramedic, being invited into family's homes during their most desperate times, their hour of need, far outweigh any of the mentioned trivial political inconveniences. Because when you deal with life and death on a regular basis and you witness the heartache and devastation this life can bring, perspective comes into play, and all of a sudden it just doesn't matter that you're finishing an hour late or that you can't watch the Queens speech on Christmas day. You really just don't give a shit, because you and your family are happy and healthy. Besides just not giving a fuck that your dinner is taking longer than you'd expect in a restaurant, or you've been put on hold for the fifth time whilst on the phone to your mobile phone provider, is so damn refreshing.

The look of relief on people's faces when you and your crew mate arrive in an ambulance at their house is something no amount of money can ever buy; it's a look that can't be mistaken for any other. In their desperation, fear and confusion, they look to you. What a privilege. We don't work miracles, we just arrive on scene, are kind, and perform skills anyone can learn. The hard bit is the mindset... and not going stir crazy.

CHAPTER THREE:

It's How You Deal With Failure That Counts

Days like this make me wonder if I can actually do this. Do I have what it takes, or have I bitten off way more than I can chew? I panic for a moment whilst tears roll down my flushed cheeks as I drive home. But then I remind myself, it's not about failure, it's about how I deal with that failure, and learn from it that counts. Every paramedic has made a mistake once, and if they tell you they haven't, they're lying.

Today started like any other, better in fact. I was working with a student paramedic who used to be an ECA where I did my training for three years, and she also knows 'A' well. Our first job was an inter-hospital transfer to the nearest primary percutaneous coronary intervention (PPCI)* for a patient having a STEMI*. A STEMI is a heart attack, which differs from a cardiac arrest. One of the most common questions I'm asked other than 'what's the worst thing you've ever seen?' is 'what's the difference between a heart attack and a cardiac arrest?' In a heart attack, the heart still beats creating a pulse, and the patient often remains conscious, but one of their coronary arteries has become blocked, causing distal cell death to the cardiac muscle itself. This is an irreversible process and will eventually lead to a cardiac arrest. A cardiac arrest is when the heart stops beating altogether, or stops beating in a rhythm which is compatible with life, so the patient loses their pulse and stops breathing.

We transfer the patient to PPCI in a timely manner and watch as the cardiac surgeons perform live surgery. The consultant inserts a catheter- which comprises of a camera and a tiny un-inflated balloon- and a stent* into the patient's groin. The catheter, followed by the stent, then travel up the aorta and are inserted into the coronary circulatory system, where the occlusion is located, the stent is expanded and the clot obliterated. I still find this process incredibly fascinating to watch on the live hospital screen.

After the buzz of watching emergency cardiac surgery, we treated ourselves to a takeaway coffee and proceeded to the ambulance to await our next call out. We weren't waiting long though before we were sent to a paediatric having a seizure twenty miles away. I sped down the busy streets, but seconds felt like minutes, particularly when we were updated by Control that it couldn't be confirmed whether the four year old child was breathing or not. When driving to a job like that and the adrenaline's pumping and you feel sick to your stomach, you have to keep reminding yourself not to take any unnecessary risks. You'll be no use to that little girl if you crash the ambulance.

When we arrived on scene, we both breathed out loud a huge sigh of relief when we saw the little girl sat talking and playing with her mum in the nursery's first aid room, waiting patiently for our arrival. The patients mum proceeded to inform us

how her daughter has been having absence attacks*
daily for approximately one month, of which she
had two this morning, and the nursery were obliged
to dial 999. The patient is already under a
neurologist and is awaiting an
electroencephalogram (EEG)* at the end of the
week, but hasn't got a diagnosis yet, nor has she
ever had two attacks in such quick succession of
each other. For this reason, on the walk to the
ambulance for a full assessment I explained to the
mum that even if her daughter is medically fit, we'd
still be taking her to hospital due to having two
attacks in such close succession of one another and
no diagnosis. The mum agreed and to me this
treatment plan was blatantly obvious, so I stupidly
assumed my colleague also agreed. Note to self-
never to assume. It makes an 'ASS' out of 'U' and
'ME'. My crew mate has been in the ambulance
service for over ten years, as an ECA first, now a
student. She's extremely intelligent, far more than
me, and she knows it. I felt like she viewed me as
an inexperienced, perhaps incompetent paramedic,
fresh from university. I was struck by imposter
syndrome. I'm intimidated by her and I think she
could tell this, which made the coming situation
even more awkward for us both. After a thorough
assessment the student paramedic began:

"I'm sure my colleague agrees…" then looked at
me without saying another word.

"Yes I'm in full agreement" I said confidently, still
thinking we were on the same page and we were
going to be taking this patient to hospital.

"...That you can go home with your Mum" she continued, talking to the little girl.

I had no choice but to interrupt. It was embarrassing for everyone involved: myself, my ECA, and more than anyone, the poor confused mother and daughter. What was I supposed to tell the family now? That I disagreed and felt she needs ED, informing them I'm the most senior clinician, undermining my colleague? I didn't have a choice. As diplomatically as I could I said exactly that, leaving my colleague well and truly miffed, and the family still a little confused, before agreeing to attend hospital with us.

Once we dropped the patient off at majors, I thought maybe I was just being over the top. Maybe she didn't need hospital at all and I was wrong. I began doubting myself and my competencies, just as I'd suspected my crew mate had already done mentally about me. No! I said to myself, I wasn't wrong, I made a clinical decision based on knowledge and experience from university and placement for three years, and I stick by my decision.

I sat the student down and explained my insecurities during the job, but her response was not one I expected.

"No, you're wrong" She reassured me. "It's ok, we would have been fine leaving her at home, you'll get more experience".

"Just remember, you're practicing under my registration today, so in the end what I say ultimately goes" is what I should have said, but instead I insecurely uttered:

"Oh ok".

The next job was an elderly faller who could not assist herself off her floor unaided. I immediately saw the job going in a similar direction to the last when the student commented:

"Well I don't see any injuries, so I see no need for you to attend hospital".

I learnt from the last job.

"Let's see you mobilise, shall we?" I quickly interrupted.

Our elderly faller was unable, and lives alone; it would simply have been unsafe and irresponsible to leave her at home unable to mobilise to the toilet, or to the kitchen to get herself a glass of water. I quickly and unintentionally took over the whole job. In doing so, I apologised to the student and explained my rationale. I was relieved to say the least when she seemingly understood and agreed with my decision. We were back on even terms. Thank goodness! But then during the coming call outs, it became apparent that this was not the case at all. For the rest of the shift this very intelligent woman wasn't even blinking without my permission, and when I did ask for her assistance, she informed me 'she's just an ECA and the driver for the day'. I didn't once tell her that.

How bad a paramedic must I be, to not be able to work as part of a team with my crew mate in my first few weeks on the job? I should be able to take leadership without making my colleague feel isolated and defensive. I'd been so engrossed in my own practice, I forgot to take into account her emotions. Now my perfectly capable student thought she couldn't practice under my registration through fear of causing conflict or having her opinion undermined. I reminded myself to not feel so sorry for myself – I hate that – and to learn from my mistakes. However, this didn't change my colleague's behaviour and at the end of the night it all came to a head.

Again, my crew mate stood in total silence staring down at me, but this time I was totally stumped by the patient, who was not giving me clear answers to any of my questions. And to make matters even more awkward, the patient laughed to my colleague:

"I can see who's in charge here, you're just the driver are you?"

I wanted the ground to swallow me up.

I immediately noticed abnormal vital signs on our 'hysterically funny' patient, however I was unsure if these were related to his chronic co-morbidities highlighted in his notes, or acute. Furthermore, the patient's mobility was poor and he wasn't giving me a straight answer whether that was normal for him or not. He didn't appear confused, he was orientated to the time, place and person, and even knew who the prime minister was- which I struggle with lately with it changing every five minutes- but he just kept going off on a tangent. Whilst performing an electrocardiogram (ECG)* my colleague finally started to speak:

"Have you listened to his chest yet?"

"Yes, all clear" I reply.

"How about read his care folder left by his carers?" she continued.

"Not yet as I'm doing an ECG, but that's a good idea, would you do that for me?"

"No. I'm just driving today" she reiterated.

I completed the ECG then read his care folder and I was totally puzzled. He had a National Early Warning Score (NEWS2)* of seven, however each and every symptom contributing to that score had a chronic justification. For example, his blood sugars were slightly elevated, but the patient is diabetic and this number was not uncommon for him. His oxygen saturations* were reduced, but again this was not uncommon for the patient with chronic obstructive pulmonary disease (COPD)*. Furthermore, he was hypertensive*, but he informed me he's not been taking his blood pressure medication for a few days. The only sign that appeared abnormal to me was his tachycardia*, at one hundred and ten beats per minute (bpm), but even then it read clearly in black and white in his care folder 'the above patient has an abnormally fast resting heart rate'. It gave no indication however, how fast that resting heart rate actually was. This patient could have actually been perfectly fit -for him- or could have been septic.

Despite the patient telling me he felt his usual self, he rung 999 for a reason- all be it the reason was unclear- so in the end I came to my senses and realised there was no way I was going to be leaving the patient at home with a NEW2s score* of seven.

I held back the tears as I still doubted my every decision though, my every sentence, even on the way into hospital. 'I am a professional for goodness sake, get a grip!' I told myself. This wasn't a particularly difficult job, and in hindsight, or a better frame of mind, I'd have known exactly what to do, but in the moment, I had zero confidence left in me after a challenging day, and I no longer trusted my own decisions.

On hospital arrival it was manic. We waited at the back of a long queue whilst a nurse made her way down the line to establish the severity of each patient. When she got to me and I start handing over she stopped me and shouted loudly for all the corridor to hear:

"A NEWS2 score of seven?! And why on earth didn't you call this in".

The entire queue stopped mid-sentence and all eyes were on me. I stuttered for a moment surprised by her tone, before I proceeded to explain my reasoning. She didn't let me get very far though before she hurried off mid explanation. This was it, my confidence was shattered into a million pieces and I just couldn't hold back the tears any longer. I left the queue telling my crew mate to remain with the patient, I could not cry in front of patients' and my fellow colleagues. As soon as I started I just couldn't stop, I was a wreck, thank goodness it was the end of the shift. I honestly couldn't have faced another human being let alone a sick patient. I tried so hard to control myself and get a grip, but the tears just kept coming, so I shut myself in a toilet cubicle away from the patients and rung 'A' to tell him I couldn't do it, I couldn't be a paramedic, I haven't got what it takes, despite the last fourteen years obsessing over it. I was a complete mess. Ten minutes later I left the cubical and walked quickly with my head down to find my patient and the student, but they were gone. I checked the cubicles and eventually found them in the resus department. I caught my colleagues eye and gestured her to come out for a second. She saw I was a mess, but when I told her I could not hand over this patient, she'll need to do it for me, she refused saying:

"You attended the job and know what's going on, you have to tell the nurses" then she disappeared onto the ambulance. I didn't see any point in waiting, it wasn't going to get better, so I walked straight into resus towards the nurses dealing with my patient and I asked them if they were ready to receive my handover. I don't know if they were just being nice or if they genuinely didn't need one, but they responded in a friendly, compassionate manner telling me not to worry, whilst one nurse put her hand on my shoulder. As soon as I left the hospital and got onto the back of the ambulance I no longer tried to hold back the tears. I think only then could I calm myself down. I explained to my crew mate that we had to go back to station and I had to speak to the manager about going home sick, there was no way I could face another patient.

"We only have half an hour left" she replied. "Let's just go back to station and not say anything, and we might not even get another job".

Luckily she was right, and at 8pm I booked off the vehicle and started my journey home.

***

I have stopped crying, but I feel more depressed than ever, so I ring 'A' back up to explain the day more rationally. I ask him:

"If I'm not a paramedic then what am I? What do I do?"

I've spent my entire adult life and most of my teenage years trying to achieve this goal, I don't have a backup plan. I feel utterly empty and inconsolable.

***

When I arrive home 'A' laughs.

"Don't be so ridiculous, it's really not that bad, you're still a paramedic and you're still a good paramedic. You've just had a bad day and need to learn from it and deal with it better next time. Tomorrow is a new day. Ok?"

I'm initially angry at him; can he not see the utter despair I'm in? Does he not believe me? But I quickly realise he's right, and yes I made a mistake, but that's not the problem. We all make mistakes, because we're human. The problem is the way I'm dealing with it. Only when I realise this the next morning do I get my shit together and arrive at work bright and early with a smile on my face, hoping I learnt my lesson.

CHAPTER FOUR:

Stroke

We have two hours left before the end of the shift with a thirty minute break yet to take, meaning if we take our break now we will more than likely finish late, as most call outs take a minimum of two hours. Therefore, it would make perfect sense to volunteer for another job, forgoing our break, in the hope we will finish on time. We're in luck! Control are more than willing to send another job over, so much so they've given us an option: A fall with unknown injuries, or abdominal pain. We cunningly opt for the closest to us in distance, which is the fall.

On arrival we are met by the patient's daughter, who begins to explain the history. Yesterday morning, approximately thirty six hours ago now, the daughter found her dad on the floor following a fall with a minor head injury. When questioned by his daughter, the patient didn't remember falling, but this is not uncommon as he suffers recently diagnosed dementia. He did however have moderate facial droop, a new onset of slurred speech and increased pain in his left hip. Despite this, the daughter assisted him back to bed with the help of his agency carers when they arrived, assuming he would simply sleep it off. In the daughters defence, her dad has had stroke symptoms previously which have subsided with no medical intervention. This leads me to believe he has most likely been experiencing transient ischemic attacks (TIAs)* which are usually warnings for a more serious stroke. Later that day, twenty four hours ago now, the daughter returned to find her father's symptoms had not improved. However as they hadn't deteriorated, still no medical advice was sought, so the patient was left alone overnight. It wasn't until his evening carer arrived and recognised the symptoms to be reminiscent of a stroke, the daughter finally dialled 999.

When we arrive, we find a ninety three year old gentleman who is indeed FAST positive. The FAST test is a tool used by emergency clinicians to determine whether a patient is having a stroke, and has now been expanded to the general public. If somebody has a deficit to one or more of the components in the FAST test, including face, arms or speech, they are FAST positive and are most likely suffering a stroke. Having said that, as a paramedic I am unable to categorically diagnose a stroke, as there are a number of other less serious conditions which can cause similar symptoms, including hemiplegic migraines* and Bell's palsy*. Therefore, I must go on my index of suspicion and the worst case scenario must be excluded first. Having said that, in this case due to the age of the patient, the mechanism of injury and the history given, I would be extremely surprised if our patient is suffering a less serious condition.

Although this would usually be a medical emergency, there is no exact onset time, and even if there was, thirty six hours of FAST positive symptoms is massively outside of the criteria for most medical interventions. Therefore, it is our policy to only transport stroke patients with an onset time of less than four hours since last being seen well, straight to the CT scanner. This is why it's paramount as soon as a patient is identified as FAST positive, whether by a paramedic or a member of the general public, treatment is accessed as quickly as possible. Time is brain* as they say.

Unfortunately, our patient is upstairs in his bedroom, with only a winding staircase connecting the upstairs to the downstairs. This means the two wheeler carry chair will be required as opposed to the stretcher, which will be extremely interesting with his left sided hip pain following his fall, in addition to his FAST symptoms, but it's our only option. Whilst my crew mate is getting the ambulance and carry chair ready I administer morphine in one of his veins to ease the pain in his suspected fractured hip, ready for transportation.

Eventually he is mobilised onto the stretcher in the ambulance, made comfortable and transported to hospital, with his daughter travelling later by car. Although hard to understand with the slurred speech, I'm having a full blown conversation with the patient about his grandchildren in the back of the ambulance, when mid-sentence he suddenly becomes silent. I'm monitoring his vital signs throughout on the screen in front of me, and nothing has changed. His heart is still beating and he is still breathing at a healthy rate, but neurologically he must be silently deteriorating. His eyes are open so I try getting a verbal response, nothing. I look into his glazed eyes with my pen torch to find a sluggish response and I can physically see the facial droop in his right lip and eye progressively deteriorating now. I wasn't going to ring the hospital to pre-alert* them of this patient, nor go on blue lights due to the length of time he's had the symptoms, but I've changed my mind. It is certainly not appropriate for him to be waiting on a bed in the corridor amongst other patients and relatives, which is where I offloaded my last patient due to no beds being available. So I attempt to ring the resus department and ask my ECA to put on the blues and twos. Damn, my phone battery has gone flat mid telephone conversation. Hopefully they got enough information to get him an emergency bed before it went silent!

We arrive in the resus department in just under seven minutes. Nice bit of driving there from my colleague, but resus aren't accepting. They inform me they can't accept with no onset time, and even if they could, they have a patient on route with breathing difficulties and they take priority. I'm angry, not at the staff who are doing a fantastic job of running the chaotic mayhem, but at the system, and the situation this poor patient has found himself in. There is no way I'm allowing this patient to wait in the corridor, even if there is nothing that can be done for him. I interrupt the staff at the nurse's station in ED and explain the situation. This time I'm lucky, they put him next in the queue and transport him onto a hospital bed in a cubicle in majors. It's not ideal, but it's a damn site better than waiting in that overloaded corridor.

After I finish handing over almost thirty minutes later we check in on the patient before we leave; we're definitely finishing late now so five more minutes won't harm. I don't believe my eyes! He's sat up speaking with one of the nurses, albeit still very slurred with facial droop, but he appears the same way we found him initially, as opposed to how he deteriorated on route. I've never seen this before in three years of training and who knows how many stroke patients I've attended to. I've seen patients deteriorate like he did many times, but none of them self resolved, sadly they all passed away or were left disabled for the rest of their lives. I leave gobsmacked, but pleased the symptoms are resolving.

We're straight back at the hospital the next morning with another patient, so whilst there I ask how our previous stroke patient is doing. Unfortunately he was found to have a haemorrhagic stroke*, and was made comfortable before passing away overnight. I want to ask the hospital staff why he appeared to recover for that brief period of time, but the nurse that was on yesterday isn't in and it's manic here today, so I don't push to find out. I just hope the daughter arrived in time to say her goodbyes as I know she wasn't driving up to the hospital straight away.

CHAPTER FIVE:
Silence

I really dislike some of these large estates! No visible house numbers and about ten different groves, closes, gardens and roads with the same name, it's like a god damn maze. What makes this particular area worse is that they've pedestrianised some of the roads, meaning there are metal bollards preventing us from using that part of the street by road. This means when we do eventually find the house we're looking for, we can't get the ambulance closer than a few hundred metres to it. We eventually decide it would be quickest and easiest to park it exactly where we are already sat and walk the distance with our oxygen cylinders, drugs bags and heavy equipment in tow. We must look like right twits, like somebody trying to carry all their shopping in, in one go, from their car parked miles away, when it's evidently clear they don't have enough hands or arm power to do so- I've been that person too many times. Finally, we arrive in the patient's bedroom, lead up the stairs by her husband. She is lying in bed, lights off, facing the wall. The call came in as a category three, thirty one year old with a query chest infection, so I'm not majorly concerned that she's lying flat and has been asleep. However, when she turns around to face us and the light is switched on, I am agog at what I see. Her cheeks are bright red, almost the same colour as her pyjamas, except for her lips and tongue which are blue, and her eyes, which are extremely dark around the lids and bloodshot. I also notice her breathing is very rapid and shallow, she is almost gasping for breath. I'm astounded that not only could this patient lie flat without becoming unconscious due to hypoxia*, but also that she has been waiting over an hour for an ambulance, as it was only graded a category three. It's certainly not the call handlers' fault, nor the husband's who dialled 999, but somewhere along the line within that phone call, information was misunderstood and the seriousness of the situation was not quite realised. I immediately put oxygen on the patient- I don't need to read her oxygen saturations to know she's hypoxic- and ask my colleague to draw up a nebuliser* whilst I auscultate* her chest. I hear nothing. Damn, is my stethoscope turned off? I go to turn it on, but realise it is already turned on. I look at the blue patient gasping and realise she has a silent chest. This means her airways are so constricted that no air is moving in or out of her lungs, so she is being deprived of oxygen and carbon dioxide is building up in her bloodstream. She is becoming acidotic*.

"Change of plan" I tell my colleague, "let's draw up adrenaline before the nebuliser."

Amongst many other things, adrenaline acts on the airways, stimulating bronchodilation*. I've never been to a silent chest case before. I was always unsure how I'd differentiate severe asthma from life threatening asthma as one requires adrenaline and one doesn't. I'm pretty certain though a silent chest indicates life threatening asthma. I cannot show my inexperience to the patient or her husband. I am like a swan, calm, unruffled and efficient on the surface, but inside my brain, my feet are kicking ten to the dozen and I'm trying to remember everything university taught me. I almost laugh out loud when the husband later congratulates me on how calm I was in the situation. Luckily, when the adrenaline has worked its magic and the nebuliser is working its way through, we hear a loud audible wheeze, that you certainly don't need a stethoscope to hear. Although that might not sound overly promising, the wheeze means the airways are open just enough to allow some oxygen in, which is a huge improvement to a silent chest. This reassures me we've now turned her life threatening asthma into severe asthma, so we can get her on the ambulance and blue light her straight to the resus department with a pre-alert. On route I suddenly realise it wasn't actually my turn to attend, it was my ECAs. I apologise, but explain when I see a time critical patient like that I go into another frame of mind, a life saving emergency mode and get on with the job in hand. I become a very different person, one most people can't believe exists when they see me crying over a good film. My ECA laughs and says they'd never have wanted to attend that job anyway, but they actually did remarkably well. A good ECA is worth their weight in gold, and my ECA today would be living in a goldmine if this were true.

The patient's condition dramatically improves on hospital arrival. Her respirations per minute are still elevated and she still has a wheeze, but only on auscultation now, and even then only a moderate wheeze. She is talking to us between breaths thanking us, telling us how scared she was at the time. A nurse even looks at her and asks if she really needs to be in resus, but when I explain that I've administered adrenaline, she can't get her into a bed quick enough. For now she's stable, and I have no doubt if it stays this way, she'll be finishing a course of antibiotics and steroids back home with her husband.

CHAPTER SIX:

Hematemesis

It's been a night of utter bollox! Patients ringing 999, but then refusing hospital; No fixed address patients (NFAs) ringing because they want our drugs to get high on; and my favourite, a woman who query fractured her toe two days ago by missing the last step, and thought that she would be seen in ED quicker if she rung an ambulance at 2am. After the daughter of the patient with the broken toe told me she could follow behind the ambulance in her car to meet her Mum at hospital, she looked at me horrified when I asked her if she can just drive her weight baring Mum to hospital herself for an X-ray. Like I'd just asked her to drive her to the other side of the country.

"You'd have to take her in if I wasn't here. Can you not just pretend I don't drive" she uttered.

Reluctantly I drove the patient and daughter to ED, but took great pleasure in telling them they can wait in the minor's waiting room like everybody else, as instructed by the nurse in charge. It's these glorified taxi jobs that make me wonder why I spent three long years at university, but then you get a real job. A job where you make a difference or save a life, which makes the months of crap just disappear. It's only then you remember why you love what you do and couldn't see yourself doing anything else.

The final job of the night is a hematemesis* patient. Nine times of out of ten, this looks a lot like coffee grounds, which is a little less time critical than fresh 'frank' blood, as it indicates a slow bleed in the gastro-intestinal (GI) tract, as opposed to an acute, ruptured blood vessel. This job is only a category three, but something just doesn't sit right with neither me nor my colleague, so we drive on blues and twos. I'm with another NQP today, which is lovely as they're in the exact same position as I am. When we arrive at the care home, we are met by two enthusiastically talkative carers in no rush whatsoever, and are shown to the patient's bedroom. On entering the room, our patient is unexpectedly a deathly white, with a vomit bowl full to the rim with frank blood -certainly not coffee grounds- and a strong metallic smell, which I've never smelt before. The laid back carers proceed to inform us that our patient has also lost some blood from her rectum, so we pull down the duvet and are even more shocked at what we find under the sheets. She has haemorrhaged. 'Some' blood?! The entire bed sheet is covered head to toe in fresh pooling blood, millimetres from dripping off the mattress and onto the white carpet. Both myself and my colleague go into a time critical state, so when I quickly turn to ask the carers for assistance, I am surprised to see they have both disappeared. I shout for them whilst measuring for a blood pressure and watch as my crew mate cannulates to start a saline infusion. Her blood pressure is 55/30. Normal is around 120/80. I'm astounded she's even conscious! No wonder she's so pale, she's in hypovolaemic shock*. The carers eventually come dawdling in, so I leave my crew mate to get a line in, whilst I get the stretcher and full extrication kit. This care home doesn't have a lift and we're on the top floor.

The carer is instructed to retrieve the patient's notes and regular medications to take with us to ED. I hand equipment to the other care worker who's assisting me, asking him to take it to my crew mate, as I cannot carry it all up the stairs alone. Then he disappears into the home with our kit, whilst I get the stretcher ready. When I arrive back in the patient's room with an extrication board -it is imperative we keep the patient in the horizontal position to prevent cardiac arrest- I'm surprised to find none of our equipment which I handed over to the carer. Nor neither members of staff. My crew mate stares at me confused, as if to say 'where the fuck is the rest of the kit??' Moreover, the patient is so peripherally shut down he cannot find a vein to cannulate, so we decide to swap and he locates the carers whilst I get a line in. Yes! I get it in first time, my moment of glory and slight pride, but in all honesty it's just luck. All paramedics can cannulate and some veins are easier than others. Finally, the two carers and our kit return; in all fairness to them, they are the only two members of staff looking after the entire care home tonight. As charming as they are, it soon becomes clear to us they are still blissfully unaware of the severity of this patient. We still haven't got care notes, nor regular medications, but we don't have time to wait. Between the four of us, we carry our extremely sick patient down the care homes spiral staircase, desperately trying to keep her flat, seeing as her blood pressure is not yet improving.

Finally, we get her safely on the ambulance, and she still has a pulse. So whilst my crew mate runs to retrieve all our equipment, I ring ED to alert them of our coming arrival. Meanwhile whilst the carers wave goodbye, one states:
"I'll see you back here later today".

I assume he didn't notice the trail of pooling blood dripping from her room to our ambulance then? The patient is not so oblivious to the severity of her condition though, as she asks me if she's going to die, whilst tears roll down her pale, clammy face. It makes my heart wrench for a second, I can't lie to her. So I explain we're going to do everything within our power to prevent that from happening, but I would advise she lets us ring her next of kin to explain the situation. She nods. When my colleague returns and asks the patient what her blood type is so resus can get an infusion ready, I quickly get into the driver's seat. Within ten minutes we arrive at hospital, which I'm pleased with, but we're nowhere near out of the woods yet, as this is a small county hospital, and this patient requires a major trauma centre (MTC) and immediate surgery.

Within minutes of arriving in resus, we are surrounded by about twenty members of hospital staff: consultants, ED nurses, intensive care unit (ICU) doctors, anaesthetists and nurse sisters. I am in utter awe of them whilst I watch them working tirelessly, trying to keep the patient alive for a transfer to a better equipped hospital. When we are asked to facilitate this transfer, we say yes without any hesitation and inform our Control of the plan. While the patient is being injected with tranexamic acid (TXA)*, is being pumped unlimited pints of blood transfusions back into her circulatory system, and is covered head to toe in heated blankets to manage her hypothermia, I go outside to ring her daughter. It's 4:30am, so she's initially not particularly impressed to receive my phone call, informing me she has already been made aware by the care home and will visit her mother later this morning. However, when I explain the urgency of the situation as diplomatically as I can over the telephone, she wakes her husband immediately and frantically asks him to drive her to the hospital. When I return back in resus, the patient is back on the ambulance stretcher with kit I've never seen, let alone used before, hanging off all four corners of the bed. I'm mildly concerned as I don't know how to use any of this advanced equipment and I'm not authorised to administer blood products, however before I get a chance to say anything, an ICU consultant informs me he'll be travelling in the back of the ambulance with us, along with an ED nurse. What a relief! So I quickly put all of our kit back in the truck, dumping the extrication board in the side cupboard filthy in blood, until we get back to station and clean out the entire truck later. As I attended the last job, its technically my crew mates turn to attend, but on these sort of jobs you can't have enough hands, so we both attend, working collectively as a team to provide the most effective and efficient outcome for the patient. This does however mean that I have to drive this patient an hour to the major trauma centre, with an ICU consultant, nurse, my colleague and a seriously ill patient in the back, on blue lights. Of course I've driven on blues hundreds of times before, but not yet with a patient in the back, let alone a dying patient and their consultant. I need to find the right balance between speed, which I'm well aware this patient needs, and not driving so fast I knock my colleagues over in the back, whilst they're trying to stabilise our patient. My hands are glued to the wheel, I have to keep rubbing the sweat off them and onto my trousers every five minutes. Luckily, this is my last shift in a set of four nights, so my uniform is due a good wash.

Finally, after what feels like hours, we arrive in just under fifty minutes. Thankfully at this time in the morning there's very little traffic on the roads, and we made it without the patient arresting on us. Thank the lord! As there was very little we could have done had her heart have stopped beating on the back of our ambulance this morning. We could give her all the CPR in the world but that won't plug the holes.

After transferring the patient straight into theatre, I walk back to the ambulance with a filthy stretcher, but a massive smile on my face and adrenaline pumping through my body, knowing I just helped save a life. We all worked as a team to actually save someone, and believe it or not, we don't get to do that very often. I can't stop smiling on the way back to station, we even stop for coffee with the nurse and consultant to debrief. This is the NHS, each and every member of staff from cleaners to paramedics to top surgeons, working as a team to save a life; without any of which, the outcome may not have been so positive.

I sleep so well that day, until around 3pm. I was so tired once the adrenaline wore off, I can't even remember driving home. I check my emails to see if a position has become available where I trained yet, and I'm deflated by the email I actually find. It reads as follows:

"Georgia,

The day shift found the scoop covered head to toe in blood after your final call out this morning! Can you imagine what would have happened if that had have been required on another job and not checked? Photos were taken of the mess and I was almost tempted to email them to the entire station. I resisted on this occasion. Come and find me in my office at your earliest convenience."

I'm utterly mortified and disappointed in myself, so much so, when I try telling 'A' about it I can't get the words out because I can't stop crying. It's funny, when I put my uniform on I'm solid (usually). I'm not easily emotional or sensitive, I'm a rock, but as soon as I'm home and I relax, I'm normal Georgia again, I cry at such little things- and big things, like datix's. I certainly won't make this mistake ever again. A few days later though, the blow is eased by an email from the ICU consultant congratulating me and my crew mate on saving a life, and I realise, if not cleaning a piece of equipment is the only thing I did wrong on that job, then I think I did alright.

CHAPTER SEVEN:

DOA

Today I'm working with a lady who was on the same emergency driving course as me when we first started our jobs, only four months ago. We had some really great banter whilst nervously tearing down the high streets, feeling like gods as the traffic parts for us, as we are having today. I love these shifts, it doesn't feel like work, it feels like two old girl friends driving around town, assisting anyone who needs it. We were only just talking about cardiac arrests, in that she hasn't been to one yet, and guess what, we get a category one come in, reading: 'not breathing, CPR in progress'. We floor it there, and luckily as it's only five minutes away, we get there in two. It's a very narrow road, with queuing traffic now behind us, so we park where we can, grab all our kit and hurry into the house. Its further away than we think, and these bags are not light! Initially nobody answers, so we let ourselves in through the unlocked front door and shout 'ambulance'. It's only after three or four shouts a man in his late sixties, teary eyed, comes running down the stairs crying:

"She's at the top, she's at the top".

It's a three story house and she's up a very narrow staircase on the top floor -why are they always on the top floor? We try to hurry, but don't want to injure ourselves on these dangerously narrow steps. We'll be no good to anyone then.

The call had come in as an eighty eight year old, but there is no way this man's wife lying on the hard floor is eighty eight. It later transpires she's actually fifty eight. Unfortunately, the patient has been deceased for many hours, most likely losing consciousness late last night or the early hours of this morning, as she is as cold as ice and is in rigor mortis. It's a DOA*. She lays supine next to her bed, eyes closed, face peaceful and arms crossed, which all make me think she died acutely in her sleep, with no pain or struggle. Due to her being in rigor mortis and her arms being crossed, I initially struggle to apply the defibrillator pads onto her chest and listen for heart and lung sounds for two minutes with my stethoscope - protocol for every corpse, to confirm death- but with my crew mate's help, we get the checks we need. After confirming there is no carotid pulse* and that pupils are fixed and dilated, we both proceed downstairs to inform the grieving husband. Seeing dead bodies doesn't faze me anymore, in fact emotionally I feel nothing; that's what the job will do to you. But seeing and informing grieving family does do something to me inside. I get that wrenching, almost ripping sensation in my abdomen. As we walk into the living room to greet the husband, I don't have to say a word, he already knows.

"I'm so sorry for your loss" I empathise.

He proceeds to tell us how he has been married forty years and they were due to board a cruise ship this morning to celebrate their wedding anniversary. In fact, he had just gone upstairs to wake her to excitedly inform her they need to leave soon before they missed their taxi, when he found her unresponsive. This even tugs at my heart strings. After I've explained what happens next, we await the police who act on behalf of the coroner. This can take up to two hours, and I'm not going to pretend I don't struggle to make light conversation in these situations for that long, especially when they refuse a hot -or cold- drink. The three of us sit in silence for a moment then myself and the husband start talking at the same time.

"Go on" he says.

"No really, it's not important, you go" I reply.

"Ok, I've changed my mind, I will ring my daughter after all if that's ok?' he utters.

"Of course it's ok!"

His daughter lives abroad where it is currently the middle of the night. He didn't want to call her at first through fear of waking her in a panic, but I reassure him I'm sure she'll understand. He agrees, but declines my offer of ringing on his behalf.

"It would be better coming from me" he assures.

His hands shaking, he picks up the phone and starts dialling the number.

"I hope I've dialled it correctly" he mutters.

"Yes, you wouldn't want to ring a stranger and tell her that her mother's died" I laugh, trying to make light of the situation.

Thank goodness he didn't seem to notice this comment, as he didn't even bat an eyelid. My crew mate definitely did though and quite rightly glared at me, as if to say 'did you really just say that?' I really do struggle making light conversation. The daughter doesn't answer despite numerous attempts, but other family members do when called. Each answering joyfully:
"Oh we were just talking about you two" or "when are you leaving for your cruise then?" before continuing on their conversations. He has to interrupt, stuttering:

"Well… actually… we're not going, she's passed away' his voice breaking. On the other end of the phone is a painful deafening silence, each and every time, for what must have felt like minutes, before:

"Oh my god, I'm so sorry, oh my god" comes.

This phrase is repeated numerously by multiple family members. People never really know what to say in these situations, partly through grief and shock, but partly because they know nothing they say will make it any better. Nothing will ease the victims grief in this difficult time, so you just have to be there for them, be a shoulder to cry on, someone to trust, who they can express their full emotions with. That's what they'll remember. Soon after these dreaded phone calls are made, the police arrive, who reiterate to the husband they are only there to act on behalf of the coroner. The police usually handle it from here, so we go to the ambulance to print the recognition of life extinct (ROLE) document. I've seen the printer used before of course, but in blind arrogance and utter stupidity, I've never attempted to use it myself. So here we are, a pair of new life saving clinicians, staring blankly at a black box which calls itself a printer. We can't help but laugh as we press print then stare at it intently, watching as nothing happens. There are no buttons or screens, just a rectangular hole for paper to be extracted. I'm baffled. My ECA suggests ringing management. I can't do that! What will they think of me? That I'm incompetent! Luckily, in a final attempt to make it work, I try turning the engine on in the cab, and voila! It prints five copies. I hand the copies to the police officer on re-entering the scene and notice they're all enjoying a cup of tea! I did try and offer the husband multiple cups!

On leaving scene I can't help but think how unfair it is. Fifty eight years old is so young nowadays, and the only co-morbidity she had was hypertension* which she took medication for. She lived a healthy lifestyle, exercised often and didn't smoke or drink alcohol. How was this fair? I also realise my ECA still hasn't been to a working arrest yet.

CHAPTER EIGHT:

Dreams

After a long day of nail biting, lifesaving intervention including itchy feet, first menstrual cycles and a blocked nose, we are finally sent to a stroke. At last a proper job, something that reminds me why I spent three arduous years at university. I'm not ashamed to say I look forward to these jobs, the more serious the better. Not because I want anyone to go through this hell - I'd never wish that on my worst enemy - but unfortunately it's inevitable, it's going to happen whether I like it or not. So rightly or wrongly I want to be there when it does happen, to provide support and reassurance; and perhaps selfishly, use procedures I've been longing to perform since I was taught them. People tell me I must be a special kind of person to be a paramedic, and they're right, but not in the way they think! I regard myself as a different kind of special, bordering on pathologically insane sometimes- particularly after a set of night shifts. But you ask any front line clinician and they'd all say the same, we have to be. I mean who chooses to be covered in bodily fluids daily?

When we arrive at scene and the patient answers the door, he doesn't particularly look like someone having a stroke, but I'm not going to make my clinical decision based on initial impressions. He leads us to his living room where his daughter is sitting and we all take a seat when instructed.

Normally at this point we are bombarded with the patient's life history, including their appendectomy* fifty years ago and what they had for tea last night, but here we are all looking at each other in silence.

"So how can we help?" I ask.

"I'm not sure really" the patient replies, and here we are, sat in silence again.

"What's happened?" I ask the daughter.

"Well, Dad's been confused".

I don't seem to be getting any more information than this out of either of them, so whilst my ECA performs a full set of vital signs and an ECG, I perform every neurological test I know, from the cranial nerves to a mini mental state examination (MME). This is partly to exclude a stroke and other acute neurological deficits, but also to bide myself some thinking time whilst I decide what to do next. He passes with flying colours, and his vital signs are perfect, so I realise the only way I'm going to find out what's wrong with this patient is by taking a history, and it's worse than getting blood out of a stone!

"I've been having bad dreams" the patient confesses.

"In your sleep?"

"Yes, yes he calls me up to tell me when he wakes up" the daughter interrupts.

"I'm not confused though" the patient argues.

"Well no, no, not confused" the daughter stutters, "I just feel so sorry for him having these bad dreams in the night when I'm not there with him, so I drive over to see him. I just feel so guilty I haven't been there for most of my Dad's life".

She then proceeds to enlighten me on how she lost touch with her father in her teens and only got back in touch with him five years ago. Since then she's been trying to make up for lost time. It was recently after she got back in touch with him five years ago, these nightmares started.

"So, when you arrive at your father's house he's back to normal? Not confused?" I ask.

"No, he's fine" she tells me abruptly.

I desperately try to get a better history without asking leading questions or patronising them, because surely someone wouldn't ring at 16:30 for having nightmares for the last five years, would they? I ask numerous questions including 'how often are these occurring?' 'Are they at the same time every night?' 'Does anything make them worse or better?' and 'do you ever have them whilst you're awake?' He doesn't. And I'm getting nowhere. I'm partly asking these questions in the hope the patient might disclose something that seems insignificant to him but is the final piece of the puzzle which makes it all make sense for me. This doesn't happen. And again, partly to work out what the hell to do next with this patient. I am stumped and turn to my ECA in the hope it's just me that hasn't got a clue what's going on, but as soon as I look to him for support, he shrugs his shoulders and tries to hide a laugh under his breath. I'm convinced there's got to be more to this than an elderly gentleman having nightmares whilst he sleeps. For five years! With no deterioration and an overly concerned daughter. Unbelievably though, after polite conversation for over an hour, it just so transpires this is exactly the case, and unsurprisingly he is not having a stroke. Another fun filled day in the ambulance service!

CHAPTER NINE:

Irony

We've just booked onto the only ambulance left on station, and it's a mess. That's the problem with starting at 10:00, it's first come first serve and all the good ambulances are gone. In fact, sometimes there isn't even an ambulance for us to book onto if we're a truck down, so I guess we should think ourselves lucky- or unlucky, depending on how you look at it. Just as we check it over and discover the reversing camera is broken, the side step doesn't deploy unless you give it a good kick, and the stretcher looks like it's been recycled from a 1970s vehicle, we get a job. We haven't finished our vehicle daily inspection (VDI) yet, so we could potentially be going out on a truck with no oxygen, cannula's or diesel! Although this is unlikely, as every member of staff is required to restock and top up fuel at the end of their shift. Having said that, we've all got onto a filthy ambulance before, where sharps are cascading over the lid that won't close, and there's not enough kit to even manage the common cold, let alone an arrest. The only thing I am sure of is the drugs which I signed out myself on arriving this morning. We hop into the cab and notice it's a category one, so start making a move on blues whilst we remind Control we haven't finished our VDI.

"I know, I'm sorry guys, but you're the only recourse available, and there has been a rollover road traffic collision (RTC) involving two casualties, both trapped in the vehicle, unknown whether conscious and breathing."

I've been to plenty of RTCs before but the patients have always been deceased, with injuries incompatible with life, or have extricated themselves with no harm done. Could today be the day I'm in charge of a time critical trauma patient, on the brim between life and death? I'm nervous, but excited. Will I finally get a chance to use the lifesaving trauma procedures I learnt at university? I'm sure I fit the NQP stereotype perfectly, like a trauma craving, blood thirsty machine. 'Trauma, trauma trauma! What? Where? When? Helicopter emergency medical service* (HEMS?!). WOW!'

When we arrive on scene, I'm surprised to see another ambulance and HEMs, as I thought it was just us. I throw on my Hi-Viz and helmet and rush to the scene. The car is crumpled and on its side. I can hear a young woman inside the vehicle crying out in fear and pain, but I can't see anything over the vast number of bodies trying to assist her, including fire crews, HEMs, road paramedics and army personnel. My colleague identifies me in the crowd and tells me not to worry, they've got it covered, but to attend the patient who self-extricated and laid himself down on the grass. I turn to see a male in his mid-thirties laid flat at the side of the carriageway, laughing and messing about with his army mates. Selfishly, my ego is utterly deflated and I walk to the probably uninjured patient, fuming. However, by the time I reach him I have a more professional, polite manner. My ECA proceeds to tell me how relieved he is we got this patient and not the other one. Well, that makes one of us. The patient doesn't appear to be in too much pain when we crouch next to him and introduce ourselves. As his colleagues disperse though, the expression on his face changes and he whispers in my ear:

"Please can I have some pain relief, it's agony, but I don't want the lads to see".

Suddenly, I feel the utmost sympathy for him.

"Of course! But first I need to know the extent of your injuries as that dictates what I can give you, where is your pain?"

"My shoulder and lower lack" he reports.

Once I exclude cervical vertebrae spinal (C spine) tenderness, head injury, neurological and circulatory impairment and respiratory trauma, I give him a choice.

"We need to immobilise your back which means gently rolling you onto our spinal board. We can either do that now and get you on the ambulance where we'll then give you analgesia*, or we can give you the analgesia now to help with the pain of the extrication?' He swallows his pride.

"Fuck it, just get me the pain relief now, it's agony".

Getting to his chest, neck and head was easy, but getting to his upper arm in his four thick layers will not be so much. Whilst he inhales Entonox* deeply, myself and my ECA attempt to pull his arm out of his sleeve. He cries out in pain.

"This isn't going to work, we're going to have to cut it off" I sigh.

The patient looks at me in disbelief and goes a deathly white.

"The coat" I reassure him "not the arm".

"Oh thank god" he cries.

It's funny how people's imaginations get the better of them when they are scared. His sergeant isn't too happy that I'm cutting into his expensive army gortex jacket to cannulate, but when I explain that if I administer drugs orally there is a chance he may vomit whilst strapped to the spinal board, which will cause much worse unnecessary complications, he understands. All his mates have reappeared now, but he doesn't seem to mind anymore seeing as he's as high as a kite on Entonox. In fact, he even tells me the reason he joined the military was for the banter.
"Are you gonna have to cut his pants off too? Ah, please do" one of them laughs.
They all cheer at this remark, including the patient. This keeps him distracted and in high spirits whilst I cannulate, administer morphine, an antiemetic*, and immobilise him onto the spinal board; then into the ambulance. By this point the other patient has also been extricated and immobilised, and is travelling to the same hospital as us. She can't be too badly injured then as she's not travelling to a major

trauma centre. On route to ED I reassure my patient it is very unlikely he has fractured his spine, as only approximately five percent of people with back pain following trauma have actually fractured their spines. And I'm confident that he mobilised himself out the car, and was walking across the grass unaided.

"It's all just precautionary, but only x-rays will tell for sure." I tell him.

As I leave the patient in the safe hands of ED and wish him and his family all the best, we head back to station to finish the VDI. He really is a lovely, genuine man. It's only later that day when admitting another patient to ED, I discover the extent of his injuries. He has fractured two of his lumbar vertebrae and his scapula* in half! And I told him it was all just precautionary! He's very thankful for all our help and doesn't seem to mind I wasn't convinced it was broken when I go to visit him, but that doesn't make me feel any less guilty and sorry for this poor man. He will likely never work on the front line again. I'm even more gobsmacked though, when I later find out the other patient who was trapped in the vehicle, was discharged earlier today with just some minor bruising. The irony!

CHAPTER TEN:

Busiest Night Of The Year

It's my first New Year's Eve as a paramedic and I'm strangely excited. Surely only people who are genuinely sick will ring 999 tonight? And I imagine they'll be a lot of them. I used to visualise myself working as a paramedic over New Year, tearing up the streets in my decorated ambulance, adrenaline pumping, saving a live at midnight. Off course it's really not as glamorous as that though! I think I have watched too many films.

I always thought it would be the busiest night of the year, so I'm highly surprised that one hour into the shift, we're still sat at the station awaiting our first call out. I'm certainly not complaining though, as the communal area is filled with pigs in blankets, alcohol free mulled wine, chocolate, fig rolls, pretzels and bottles and bottles of pepsi max. And I have no-one telling me not to devour as much as my stomach will allow.

After another hour of engulfing all I can consume before I vomit, I hope to god we're not sent to a cardiac arrest. There's absolutely no way I could perform CPR without retching or getting a stitch. Just as I sit my greedy ass in the reclining chair though, the radio goes off, and it's a concern for welfare. Fuck. This could very easily turn out to be an arrest, so I force my bloated body into a standing position and hobble my way to the ambulance. The screen reads: 'Elderly woman trapped behind the front door of her property in assisted living, screaming for help'. This is only a category three call but we both agree it sounds pretty horrific for the elderly patient and the helpless neighbour, so we hurry to the scene. On arrival, we are met by a middle aged gentleman going out of his wits trying to unlock the patient's front door now he's finally found the master key. Fortunately, he succeeds, and the three of us enter the property as quickly as we can to identify the cause of all the screaming. My colleague jokes 'she's probably just found a huge spider in the bath'. As he opens the door though his face drops and he mumbles 'oh fuck' under his breath, followed by the neighbour who has a very similar response. I'm nervous for a moment at what I might to find. If the ECA who was in army for over twenty years is shocked by what he's seen, I think I should be worried. Luckily as I have some horrific image set it my mind though, I am pleasantly surprised to see the actual damage. There is a lot of blood, but her head isn't hanging off, as I'd imagined by the men's initial responses. I breathe a heavy sigh of relief. Earlier this evening the patient had been mobilising across the living room to pour herself another shandy ready for midnight, when she tripped on her rug and landed on her hard marble fire place. I think she got a bit confused though, as it was still only 21:00. She didn't lose consciousness but couldn't mobilise, so all she could do was shout for help, until eventually a neighbour heard her. During this time, blood had wept from her cranium and oozed down her face and neck onto her clothes, leaving her masked in a layer of dried red, with only the whites of her eyes untouched. I can see how it looks pretty horrific to my crew mate and the neighbour. On first inspection she does look like she must be a seriously wounded casualty at a major aeroplane collision, or collapsed building or something similar, I suppose. Once we apply direct pressure to the wound though and clean her up, everything is much calmer and less dramatic. There is no disputing however, that she has caused herself either a venous or arteriole* bleed, so time is still of the essence. Not because she will lose enough blood to go into hypovolaemic shock -we can manage the bleeding with a trauma dressing- but because an impact that hard to her skull could have easily caused an internal haemorrhage we cannot identify without a CT scan; particularly as she has been drinking, and the effects of alcohol will mask the symptoms of a cranial bleed. On route to ED we reassess, reassess and reassess some more. Symptoms are not always apparent immediately, so it is vital we repeat our assessments and vital signs to ensure we haven't missed anything. Fortunately, everything apart from her drunken manic state and open head wound revealing her skull, appears within normal parameters on ED arrival. So we leave the patient in the capable hands of the resus department, and head back to station to change our blood stained clothes for our spare uniforms - and for another fig roll.

Its 23:30 and they've sent us on standby to the car park on the other side of town to await our next job!

Why couldn't they just wait half hour for us to watch the fireworks on TV and share an alcohol free mulled wine with our co-workers on New Year? Just as I go to radio them up to question their barbaric request though, an actual job comes in. It's a mental health job. These are all too familiar around Christmas and New Year. We arrive at the mental hospital ten minutes to midnight on the 31st December, and nobody seems to be answering the door. What is most frustrating though, is we can see the staff through the glass drinking their makeshift bubbly, socialising and laughing. They're all just facing in the opposite direction and can't hear our knocks over their loud music. It's not even midnight yet. Eventually one of them see's us, and finds the whole thing hilarious as they lead us to the patient. We are met by a middle aged bariatric* man, who has two black eyes, one of which is bloodshot, and epistaxis -AKA a nose bleed. The nurse with him attempts to explain the situation, but it's difficult to hear between the 'fuck you's' and 'get out of my room you effing c****' coming from the patient's mouth. Eventually we gather that he was assaulted by another inpatient earlier today, as a result of his colourful language towards them, and has now informed the staff that he has lost vision in one of his eyes. I'm certain this isn't a permanent impairment, but just to be sure, he needs ED.

Just as we get ready to leave to for hospital, we hear the cheers and cries coming from the patient's little satellite television, of London seeing in the New Year.

"Happy New Year" I wish my crew mate with a smile.

"Happy New Year!" The psychiatric team and my crewmate reply, smiling and laughing.

"Happy? Fucking happy?" The patient cries. "Stop laughing will you, I've been physically assaulted and you're all laughing at me you ass holes! Go die you pieces of shit. I bet you've never seen anyone assaulted like this before".

(Happy New Year to us).

"No, we're not laughing at you sir, were wishing you Happy New Year, it's midnight on 31st of December"

"Go fuck yourself" he responds.

This is definitely not how I envisaged my first New Year's shift when I was an eager teenager. I'm pretty sure though this is probably how I'm going spend the next forty of them. It could be worse, one crew are out in an abandoned forest looking for a body that doesn't exist following a hoax call, and another's ridding their ambulance of vomit.

Towards the end of the night, I notice our first patient of the shift back in resus. I had watched them being admitted to the acute medical unit (AMU) earlier this evening, what on earth were they doing back in resus?

"Hi there" I nervously approach the consultant. "We brought this patient in last night then saw them admitted to AMU, what changed?"

"The registrar on the ward noticed the patient was becoming increasingly breathless so performed a respiratory exam. On doing so they identified surgical emphysema* over the patients left lung, so we're treating her for a rib fracture and pneumothorax*. She showed no signs of pneumothorax the entire time she was with us in the emergency department. The symptoms developed around eight hours after the injury" the consultant continues. "Don't worry though, there's no way you could have known, she wouldn't have displayed any symptoms when you were with her".

The reassurance from the respiratory consultant puts my mind at rest thankfully, as I just don't think I have the energy to panic this morning. As I get ready to sign in the drugs and drive home to my bed to celebrate my new year, I can't help but realise how quiet the night was! I was always under the illusion New Years Eve shifts were manic. The only reason for the lack of jobs I can think of, is the amazing drunk tanks scattered around town, dealing with the drunks and addicts, saving ambulances from being dispatched to them. I don't think about it for too long though, I have a week off now and I'm going to try think about anything other than work after my five consecutive, gruelling night shifts.

CHAPTER ELEVEN:
SVT

It's bitterly cold out. Black ice everywhere and intermittent hail stones, which are all fine when you're your winter climbing, or tucked up on the sofa with a hot chocolate - either just as appealing. It's not so much fun though when you're trying to drive a five ton ambulance on blue lights, sliding all over the place, on your way to a patient with palpitations and chest pain. It's getting to the point now that I'm feeling it's unsafe to continue on blue lights. I'd prefer get there five minutes late and get there in one piece than not arrive at all - a sentence that was drilled into us on the three week intense emergency driving course.

When we do arrive - and only two minutes later than predicted- the patient answers the door and leads us to her living room. I often get frustrated when the patient answers the door; if they can get up and walk to the door then they can get up and walk into a taxi, but this patient was an exception. She stumbles to the nearest chair in the living room panting for breath, before she sits down and feels her own pulse. She's a grey colour and is sweating profusely. Even if all her vital signs and ECG appear unremarkable, this one is definitely going to hospital. She just looks like a cardiac patient. No need for a thorough investigation to identify that. "It's over a hundred" she comments.

"What's over a hundred?" My crew mate asks.

"My pulse".

That doesn't remotely surprise me just by looking at her, so I immediately put on the ECG before any other piece of equipment.

"Are you in any pain?" I ask.

"Not pain, my heart is just palpating ten to the dozen and it's so uncomfortable. I can't catch my breath and it makes me feel like I'm going to faint when I stand".

When the ECG stabilises itself, it identifies a pulse of one hundred and sixty beats per minute. Again, this doesn't surprise me or my colleague in the slightest, but it does mean we need to get her to hospital quickly, if we can't slow her heart rate down here. I immediately try a manoeuvre designed for this exact situation, but as in every case I've seen so far, it doesn't prove to be effective. It rarely is effective, and colleagues that have been in the job for over ten years, claim they have only seen it work once or twice, but when there's a will -and robust evidence- there's a way, as they say. We quickly mobilise our patient into the ambulance stretcher, get a line in, just in case she deteriorates, which is highly likely, and floor it to our nearest hospital with a pre-alert. She's in supraventricular tachycardia (SVT)*. If left untreated, her blood pressure will decline, due to the heart's chambers not having enough time to refill with blood during each heartbeat, and she could eventually go into cardiogenic shock* and multi organ failure.

Alternatively, she could go into a more dangerous arrhythmia, such as VT or VF. SVTs can be caused by numerous contributing factors such as excess caffeine intake or thyroid disease, but are most commonly as a result of faulty electrical pathways within the heart itself. This is often due to fibrous scar tissue not conducting electricity well, or as a result of a congenital heart defect.

Looking at the ECG though, I'm unable to identify the cause, as the heart is just beating far too quickly on the screen to distinguish any specific abnormalities. Amazingly, we arrive in resus with no changes in vital signs. Apart from the tachycardia, her observations are all stable. We all know this won't last though, so we quickly transfer the patient from our stretcher onto the hospital bed, and complete an emergency ATMIST handover.

I'm interested in this condition, so I stick around to watch the medics at work. First, they identify the exact rhythm. Then they administer a strong emergency medicine that resets the heart by stopping it for a matter of seconds, before it spontaneously starts again; hopefully returning to a normal sinus rhythm. Almost like turning a computer off and on again when it crashes. This is an extremely tense moment for everyone involved, including me as an observer. The drug is forcefully administered and we all nervously watch as the heart rate goes from a fast, but compatible rhythm with life, into asystole- which is definitely not compatible with life. Next, we wait for a heartbeat to reappear, hopefully in a normal rhythm. For that few seconds where her heart stops beating, everyone in the room has their stomach in their mouth and stop breathing themselves for a second. I've only seen this done once before, and even though the heart was only stopped for a second or two, the sigh of relief when it began beating again was overwhelming. This is not a drug we carry, thank goodness!

As we watch in anticipation, we see the heart return to its original irregular fast rhythm. It hasn't worked. After a second ineffective dose, the next option is cardioverting the patient. Now this I've never seen, and I'm rightly or wrongly excited. Emergency electrical cardioversion, in short, involves defibrillating a patient who is still very much alive and conscious, to achieve a similar outcome. It is painful, but necessary. I'm sure the consultant in charge has performed this procedure a million and one times before, but for me, and some of the nurses crowding round the cubicle, it's a first, and we're as much nervous, as we are in awe. Even the receptionist stops for a second and watches from across the room. It all happens so quickly. The patient receives a jolt which makes her jump for a second and cry out, but as quickly as it's performed, it's over. We cannot believe it! She's still in a dangerously fast irregular rhythm, at a hundred and eighty beats per minute now. Cardioversion usually has a high success rate. This is where my pay grade ends; I am completely and utterly clueless as to how they are going to manage this patient from here on. These are the only two methods I am aware of that slow the heart down if our manoeuvres fail.

Fortunately, the consultant isn't quite as clueless as me, and uses a lot of jargon I cannot begin to understand when I ask him what the next step will be, for the decompensating patient. Then, just like that, our radio goes off for our next job. I'm gutted we don't get a chance to witness the recovery of this patient, using techniques I've never even comprehended, but we're very lucky to have stayed for as long as we did without getting another job.

Later in the shift after handing over another patient in the same hospital, I rush to the nurse in charge to find out what happened with our SVT patient. She informs me she was stabilised and is now in a normal heart rhythm, and is being monitored on a ward to prevent the rhythm from reoccurring.

CHAPTER TWELVE:

The Beach

I try not to laugh as I watch my ECA attempt to hide a retch whilst he assesses a patient's diabetic, ulcerated foot. It smells putrid and it's not a pretty sight, I'll give him that, but it is nothing compared to a call out I did as a student in my final year. Today is a wet, miserable afternoon. The job I attended was in the peak of the summer at the beach, and it had just reached thirty degrees.

Children were playing in the sea, building sandcastles and running wild, teenagers were wearing as little as they could possibly get away with, and parents were reading books whilst sunbathing on the hot sand. It looked glorious. My mentor was driving at less than five mph from the pier, trying to avoid hundreds of high spirited tourists, whilst the ECA and myself scanned the crowds for our patient. We sincerely hoped we were heading in the right direction as we were only given an estimated location, and turning round would have been completely impossible. Eventually, we identified an individual who matched the description perfectly: An NFA in his late fifties sitting on a bench on the seafront, claiming he couldn't walk. When we parked the ambulance, -I say parked, we stopped next to the bench then switched the engine off- a member of the council came running over to us, barging between members of the public, shouting:

"He can't walk! he can't walk. Here's what you need to do. You need to go get your carry chair and get him onto the ambulance. Then you need to drive him to hospital. Ok?"

Now, still to this day, when someone not medically trained tells me 'he can't walk, you're going to have to get the carry chair', my mental response is (wrongly) 'right, hold my beer, we'll get this patient walking if it kills me' (not literally).

And what do you know? On asking the patient to stand and walk onto the ambulance, he does exactly that, leaving the council worker silent and agog. At first, we all discretely smile at each other, but that was not the first time this situation has occurred. My favourite was when a community first responder (CFR) came rushing out of the patients address to tell us we need the full immobilisation and extrication kit for a patient who'd had a fall.
"Let's just see the patient first shall we" we told the CFR.

"Do you have any neck pain" I asked the patient, who'd tripped over her carpet as I palpated her cervical spine.

"No."
"Are you in any pain at all?"

"No I'm uninjured."

"Do you want to get up then?"

"Yes please" and up she gets, quite rightly, uninjured. The CFR - silent at this point - had asked her to remain still on the floor, just in case she had injured herself. This was just one CFR though. CFRs are actually worth their weight in gold, and I admire them. They volunteer to do their job, and are nine times out of ten, fantastic at what they do.

Back at the beach, our smiles were quickly wiped from our smug faces when we were hit with an comprehendible smell. It appeared to be coming from the patient's legs which were covered by numerous layers of clothing, including tracksuit bottoms and thick jeans.

"I can't feel my legs, I'm so sorry" the patient sobbed.

"That's ok, we need to have a good look at them though to see what's going on, I'm going to have to cut the layers off, is that ok?"

In doing so, the smell of rotten cabbage and decaying flesh became overwhelming, which was only compounded by the heat of the summer. We were all in masks by this point, but still couldn't hide the gags any longer. At one point I honestly thought my lunch was going to come back up, all over the patients decayed limbs. I kept apologising, but seeing as we couldn't open the ambulance doors to let some air in, due to so many crowds out there, we couldn't easily rectify the situation. Eventually when we got down to the final layer of clothing, we found black dressings and bandages covering the entirety of the patient's lower limbs. Between which was the odd glimpse of green and black flesh.

"I haven't taken these bandages off in one year" the patient confided. "They were put on my ulcers last summer by a district nurse."

We couldn't believe what we were hearing. One whole year, three hundred and sixty five days these bandages had been wrapped around his legs, so tight now, they were cutting of the bloody supply to his lower extremities.

"We better cut them off and see what we're dealing with then" my mentor joked, or so me and my ECA thought. It quickly became apparent though, this was not a joke at all.

"No, really" he continued as he saw the looks on our faces. "We need to see the extent of the condition before we can hand him over in hospital".

Dubiously, the three of us hacked away at the tight bandages and peeled away dressings which were stuck to his mangled, green skin. In many area's it was difficult to identify where the dressings ended and the skin started, as it was all covered in a yellow and green jelly-like substance I've never come across before. Unfortunately, the more bandages we removed and the more we wiped away the oozing exudate, the more white and black wax like tissue we came across, which was decayed and decomposed flesh. This was a painless experience for the patient, as he had no feeling left in these areas of his legs.

After almost an hour - with multiple breaks in between gags to get some necessary fresh air - the dressings were all removed. Regrettably though, just by smelling and looking at the exposed and decayed tissue which was once a pair of perfectly functioning legs, it was obvious he would lose them. The white indicated areas which were receiving little to no blood supply, whilst the black was necrotic tissue, which had not been perfused with oxygen rich blood for a very long time. The green jelly substance, I didn't have the foggiest, but I knew it couldn't be good.

Later that month when I went for a run along the beach, I noticed the patient again. He didn't recognise me, but I most definitely recognised him. He was back in multiple layers including jumpers, coats, jackets, tracksuit bottoms and jeans, despite the unusually warm weather. This time though, there was a difference. He wasn't sat on a bench, he was sat in a wheelchair, and the tracksuit bottoms were obviously empty from the femur (thigh) down. Just as we'd predicted, he had lost both his legs, however I was weirdly still somewhat surprised. I knew this would be the case, they were so beyond saving, but I just couldn't believe they were gone. I suppose I had just hoped that by some miracle, the doctors could save them, because I was never told otherwise. I ran the furthest I'd ever run that day. How dare I own a pair of perfectly functioning legs and not use them to their absolute fullest.

CHAPTER THIRTEEN:
Care Line Activation

We've been called to a care line activation this morning with no response. This means an elderly patient with a lifeline button around their neck - designed to be pressed in an emergency - has pressed said button, but is not responding to the care agency who are trying desperately to contact their patient via her speaker phone. This usually means one of two things: either the patient has pressed it whilst they're still conscious, and in the few moments it's taken for the call takers to respond, the patient has lost consciousness and potentially stopped breathing. Or, they've pressed it accidently and have their television volume on loud and don't have their hearing aids in, to hear the poor concerned carers. Nine times out of ten it's the latter.

On route to this elderly lady's 'concern for welfare' we notice the lanes are getting narrower and narrower and the houses grander and grander. We're really in the country now. Before we know it, we're in the middle of nowhere, not a car nor another human being for miles. Not even so much as a farm. Just two semi-detached mansions in the middle of a field. One of these houses belongs to our patient, but it's difficult to know which with no house names or numbers in sight. Eventually we find a wheelie bin with an old faded number painted on it which matches the description on our screen, so we knock on the heavy wooden door in anticipation, with no idea what we're going to find behind it. Just as my hand touches the door though it springs open, and we are met by a petite oriental lady in her late seventies, with a care line around her neck. She hasn't stopped breathing.

"ARE YOU BT?" She bellows.

"No madam, we're from the ambulance service"

"PARDON" (she doesn't have her hearing aids in)

"WE'RE THE AMBULANCE"

"OH, WELL PERHAPS YOU COULD HELP ME?"

"We'll do our best"

"PARDON?"

"SURE."

It turns out she's having technical difficulties with BT, and has no way of contacting her niece in Germany for their weekly chat. Seeing as neither myself, nor my ECA have the first clue about technological difficulties, we're both unsurprised when the breadth of our knowledge is reached by switching the router off and back on again at the plug, and the problem still isn't resolved; so we contact Control as we have no signal to call BT ourselves. They say they'll look into it. People think paramedics are life savers. Actually, we're social workers, vets, councillors and electricians. And the list goes on.

"I'll go see if I can get some signal on my phone outside" I suggest

"PARDON" cries the patient

"I'M GOING TO TRY FIND SOME SIGNAL"

"OH NO YOU WON'T" the partially deaf patient laughs. "THERE'S NO SIGNAL FOR A FIVE MILE RADIUS DEAR. IF YOU GO TO THE TOP OF THE HILL IN THE NEXT VILLAGE, YOU'LL GET ONE BAR UP THERE".

She's right! Not a single bar on her entire plot of land. With Control still not getting back to us, we decide to knock on her only neighbour's door to see if they'll kindly allow us to use their landline, in a final attempt to contact BT. They take a long time to answer, considering we can hear a gentleman chattering away to himself just the other side of the makeshift plank of wood which he seems to be using to get in and out of his home. When he does eventually open the door, we are greeted by an unkempt elderly man, also in his late seventies. He has dried food around his mouth, beard and his clothes, long matted grey hair, and is wearing a pair of tartan dungarees covered in dog hair, which look and smell like they are also covered in urine.

"Who are you?" He shouts aggressively in a thick accent.

"Morning Sir, we're from the ambulance service. We were wondering if you'd be so kind as to help your neighbour in allowing us to…"

"I ain't doing nuffin for 'er" he interrupts. "She's a fascist and a liar, she put my dog in 'er loft I'll have you know. No, I ain't doing nuffin for that crazy old bat, and neither should you! You 'ear me?"

In short, he doesn't allow us to use his phone. Just as my ECA and I try getting some inspiration from one another on what to do next, Control radio's back to us. "Right, I've contacted BT and given them the address for the patient. You can tell her they'll hopefully be there later today" The call handler informs us, understandably sounding particularly uninterested by the whole situation.

Thank goodness, problem solved. As we get back into the cab and drive off, we can't help but laugh out loud at the almost unbelievable call out. What just happened? On the way to the next job - after being thoroughly disappointed that my phone wasn't flooded with messages when we regained signal at the top if the hill - Control radio's us back up.

"BT have rung us back" they comment "And she's not a BT customer"

We can't go back now, we're on our way to a chest pain.

CHAPTER FOURTEEN:
Long Lie

Being a paramedic isn't always what people imagine. It's certainly miles apart from what I envisaged as an eager teenager desperate to save the world. The first job of the night is all too common. A non-injury elderly faller, or 'Nan down' in crew room slang. Unacceptably the job has been waiting five hours, as every ambulance allocated has been diverted to a higher category patient, who required an ambulance immediately to prevent harm to life. But now, after five long hours the call has been quite rightly upgraded from a category three to a category two, due to the elongated time frame that the patient has been waiting on a hard floor.

Once eventually gaining access to the property after dubiously rummaging around the patient's pot plants to locate his hidden front door key as instructed, we are met by an excited, unruly Jack Russell. The stench of both canine and human faeces, leftover rotten food and cigar smoke immediately hits me and my crew mate as we enter the scene. Unfortunately this is not an uncommon sight, particularly in the elderly generation who have no family, friends or support network in place, and often suffer undiagnosed dementia. Further along the hall lays a frail man in his late seventies, positioned flat on his back, unable to mobilise himself to even a sitting position. He doesn't appear remotely phased that he has had to wait five hours for an ambulance to arrive though, and even starts cracking jokes before we get a chance to apologise for such a long delay. By the time my colleague and I have helped mobilise the patient to his reclining chair, the three of us are in tears of laughter in response to his witty sense of humour. How could such an optimistic, genuine gentleman who once fought in the war have slipped through the net and be exposed to such poor living conditions? On full assessment he is medically fit, with no injuries from his mechanical fall*, tripping over his oversized rug. Additionally I am not concerned about a long lie*, as he has been rolling around his lounge in a desperate attempt to reach the phone and self mobilise. He is refusing ED attendance anyway.

I am now left feeling stumped as an overly optimistic, physically well gentleman is blissfully unaware of his unsafe living environment and I need to gain his permission to put in an emergency social services and safeguarding referral. Although I have a duty of care, our patient has full mental capacity so if he is refusing ED, and now refuses a referral, there is nothing I can do.

Although he feels it's unnecessary and a waste of NHS resources, fortunately he agrees to the referral, so will be contacted by the relevant safeguarding team and his GP in the next few days. Sadly with the rise in mental health and a reduction in funding, these call outs are increasing day by day. Hopefully the temporary inconvenience of a fall means a more permanent fix.

CHAPTER FIFTEEN:

Faulty Equipment

We're backing up another crew from the same station as us for our first job this evening. We're a little unsure why we're back up though, considering it's a category four. I can only but think it's either been categorised wrong and is actually more serious than originally triaged, or it will involve some serious heavy lifting. On arrival we are met by a bariatric disabled lady stuck in the upright position, leaning against her broken reclining chair. I knew it. The chair's motor seems to have stopped working, meaning she cannot recline the chair to a sitting position, so she is fixed like this. My paramedic colleague is on the phone getting obviously irate, so the ECA explains the situation. The patient was discharged from hospital earlier today and transported home by the patient transfer service (PTS), due to an inability to drive and no local friends or family. The PTS driver assisted her to her living room, where he then left before she had attempted to sit down. It was here the patient identified the controls had stopped working in her bariatric electric chair, and was stuck, leant in the upright position. First, she pressed her care line, who arranged for a district nurse to visit later in the day. A few hours later a district nurse did arrive, but informed the patient there was absolutely nothing they could do, so told her to await a phone call from occupational therapy (OT). Unfortunately, it got to

6 o'clock this evening and our patient had not received a single phone call, so in a panic, she dialled 999.

Now this patients chair is not just her chair, it's her bed, her security and her independence; and with it being a Friday evening, no one that can resolve the issue is open until Monday morning. This means she will be trapped in this position, day and night, over the entire weekend. We can't leave her like that! And what's more, it's her birthday!

When my colleague finishes on the phone to the district nurses with no luck, we all have another attempt at fixing the chair ourselves. We read instructions on Google and watch mechanical video's on YouTube, but no luck. It quickly becomes apparent that it's going to take a trained mechanic who specialises in these pieces of equipment to get it working again. After scanning the internet for what feels like hours, we finally find an emergency contact line for the company who makes and produces these chairs. Yes! This could resolve everything. Despite explaining the entire situation to the company though, they inform us the engineers only work 9-5 Monday to Friday, and we wouldn't get an appointment for at least a week. I struggle here not to ask him 'what the bloody hell is the point in having an emergency telephone number then?!' But I refrain.

In a final attempt to keep this medically fit patient out of hospital, we try to arrange a star bed. A star bed is an emergency spare bed, usually in a nursing home or care home, designed for temporary use in these very situations, where a patient is not safe enough to be left at home alone. Usually these are dementia or physically disabled patients when their sole carers are admitted to hospital. Or are the family carers of Alzheimer's patients who are at risk due to increasing violence; but there's a first time for everything. Actually getting a star bed though is like gold dust, and our low expectations are quickly met when we eventually receive a phone call to say nothing is available at this time. This means the only option left to us is frustratingly back to hospital. The patient is just as frustrated as we are, but there is no way we're going to leave her like this alone for the weekend, so together we mobilise the thirty five stone patient into the back of my colleague's ambulance. I feel hugely relieved it's their ambulance and not ours, as I wouldn't have the foggiest idea on where I'd start in handing this one over in ED.

CHAPTER SIXTEEN:

Status Epilepticus

When arriving on scene to a thirteen year old having a seizure at her school, it's immediately clear she's GCS three*. There's a lot of stigma around teenage girls in particular having pseudo seizures, now known as non-epileptic seizures, as a result of functional neurological disorder (FND)*. These patients are fully alert during and between their fits, and have none of the classic symptoms of a stereotypical seizure, which include incontinence, tongue biting and hypoxia; so emergency medication is not required. These seizures come from a different area of the brain and are often triggered by an underlining mental health condition. I remember one non epileptic seizure patient I went to not so long ago. An eighteen year old and her mum were raging by the fact a consultant had told her to buy a dog and get on with her life.

It's immediately clear my patient today though is not pseudo fitting. She has already been incontinent and is beginning to seize again, for the third time now, a teacher tells us. As the fit continues the patient's lips become more and more cyanotic, so I instruct my ECA to hurry out to the ambulance to get the oxygen and stretcher, whilst I cannulate. Kids are difficult to cannulate at the best of times, but kids who are mid seizure are almost impossible, so I'm silently not overly confident about this one. When I look at her arms, I see nothing, not a single blue line or protrusion, so I nervously pierce the skin blindly where I know a vein should run. Blimey! I get flashback, 'yes!' I whisper under my breath, I don't celebrate for long though. The bell has just gone for home time at the school and I look up to find myself surrounded by a hysterical mother and about thirty intrigued thirteen to fourteen year olds, all trying to peer in on the action. The teachers are trying their best to keep their students back, but we are in the middle of a regularly used corridor. The kids' chattering is so deafening, I can't hear myself think over the white noise, let alone get a history from the patient's emotional mum. So as soon as my ECA returns, we quickly extricate the teenager onto the stretcher, and into the safety and comfort of the ambulance. Comfort for me more than anything! Now I'm back in my office I can concentrate better. We can still hear the kids crowding around the vehicle, but the noise is now faded by the thick yellow metal confining us in. Just as the mum begins communicating with me, her daughter starts seizing again, for the fourth time now. I know I have to start getting drugs in, and quickly, so whilst the mum explains that her daughter does not have a diagnosis yet, but is under neurology and has been experiencing these to a lesser extent for almost a month, I frantically recheck the diazepam guidelines for a thirteen year old. I've never even cannulated a child before today, let alone administered them a controlled drug, so I'm obviously very nervous, but I try not to show it on my face in front of the concerned Mother. Ten milligrams?! That's an adult dose. I look at her and she's so petite, how could she possibly need the full adult dose? I recheck it on my drugs app, confirm it with my ECA three times, and even cross check it with my old drugs book. They all say ten milligrams, so that's what I push into her tiny vein, dubiously. I hope to god this works as we're well over thirty minutes from hospital, even on blues. Ten minutes later though, she's on her seventh seizure, and they're full blown tonic clonic* now. First her face goes bright red and she becomes as rigid as a board. Her arms and legs stretched out as far as they will reach. This is the point her lungs stop receiving any oxygen and I watch as her oxygen saturations drop from 98% to 95% to 92%. I quickly turn the oxygen up to the highest setting. Next, all of her limbs start violently shaking, as she thrashes her entire body weight onto the stretcher, making it clunk and creak. She needs more drugs, so I draw up the last of the diazepam I'm authorised to administer, and pray. The mum becomes hysterical now and I really can't blame her, it's emotional even for me to watch, and I don't even know the kid.

"The doctors don't believe me" the patients mum weeps. "They think she's faking it for attention."

I'm astounded, this is a textbook example of a tonic clonic seizure. You can't fake hypoxia and cyanosis, or the tachycardia. Nor her eyes rolling back into her cranium during each episode. The only thing you could fake I suppose is the urinary incontinence and the biting of the tongue, but why would you? In fairness though, the mum does acknowledge this is the worst she's ever seen her daughter, and the doctors very rarely actually get to witness the seizure activity, as by the time patients arrive at hospital, it has almost always subsided. So, I advise the mum to film the next seizure to show the consultant. It's extremely disturbing to watch as the patients Mum holds up the phone in her hand, but looks away as it records, weeping uncontrollably. But there's no disputing these are true seizures and this may be the only way the doctors get to witness the epileptic activity for themselves. Of course, there are many causes of seizure other than epilepsy and FND though. Common causes include head trauma, tumours, hypoxia, electrolyte imbalances*, hypoglycaemia* and poisoning, just to name a few. So, diagnosing epilepsy is a very long drawn out process, which can only be confirmed by a senior consultant when all of the above have been excluded. It's also a life changer. Epileptic patients may never be allowed to drive, or have a bath unassisted again, so doctors have to be 100% sure the diagnosis is correct.

It takes another five long, helpless minutes after the last drug administration for the patient to finally stop seizing. In those five minutes there was absolutely nothing more I could do. She'd already had all the drugs I'm authorised to administer, she's been on high flow oxygen throughout, and we're flooring it to the resus department. It could only get worse or start getting better and thank goodness, it's started getting better. On arriving at resus, she starts to come round. All be it she has no idea where she is, she is talking incomprehendably, and looks like she's just come out of a boxing ring, but her eyes are open and she's stopped seizing. Besides, it's completely normal to be confused and fatigued after a seizure or multiple seizures, so I'm not at all concerned by this. This is called the postictal phase*. As I walk into resus, I am greeted by over ten clinicians silently awaiting my clinical handover.

"Patient is a thirteen year old female who collapsed at school at approximately 15:30 and had three consecutive tonic clonic seizures, all lasting about a minute each. On ambulance arrival the patient was GCS 3…"

"GCS 3?" one consultant interrupts. "Squeeze my hands" she asks the patient, to which she complies "you see, she's not GCS 3!"

"Well, her GCS is now 13" I stutter, "It was three on our initial arrival" she looks at me in disgust, then starts assessing the patient before I finish my handover. I continue anyway as there are still another nine clinicians looking at me.

"She was in status epilepticus for further forty minutes, which only subsided once twenty milligrams of intravenous (IV) diazepam had been administered, titrated over the course of approximately thirty minutes."

"Twenty milligrams?!" She interrupts again "And how old is this patient?"
"Thirteen."

I've completely lost my trail of thought now, so I hesitantly utter any last pieces of information I feel may be relevant and leave the resus department, silently flustered and panicked. What if I gave her the wrong dose? Have I overdosed her? Oh my God, I could have killed her! I try not to cry as I recheck for the fourth and fifth time the drug dosages for a thirteen year old. Twenty milligrams it says, it's right there in black and white: IV diazepam, thirteen years old, initial dose ten milligrams, repeat dose ten milligrams, maximum dose twenty milligrams. I didn't get it wrong, and my ECA re-assures me our patient was definitely GCS 3 on our arrival. So why was the doctor so harsh on me? In her defence, it is extremely difficult to measure GCS between seizures, so next time I'll just leave the GCS aspect out of the handover, unless asked. Whilst finishing off my paperwork, a different registrar comes in to talk with me. She apologises for the tone of her colleague, who is actually an agency doctor and doesn't usually work for the hospital, before reassuring me that ambulance guidelines are different to hospital guidelines, so not to worry. When the paperwork is finalised and the ambulance ready and waiting for our next patient, I go in to see how the thirteen year old and her mum are doing. To my pleasant surprise she is sat up in bed on her phone, eyes open, talking in full, comprehensible sentences. She unsurprisingly has no idea who I am, but I couldn't care less, she looks a little tired, but like a normal, healthy teenager again.

CHAPTER SEVENTEEN:

I've Never Seen It Look Like That Before

We're heading for a rectal prolapse - not ourselves, our patient. This means the rectum has inverted in on itself and is visible from the external anus. I'm very surprised at the age of the patient though, being only twenty five. These are much more common in the elderly. That being said, twenty five year olds have been known to have heart attacks and strokes, albeit extremely rare, so nothing is impossible. We are met by the patient's boyfriend who looks about sixteen, but must be older as he is covered head to toe in tattoos and piercings. He leads us into the living room and there stood leant over the couch as far over as she can stretch, is our patient, thankfully in a long skirt. I can't take her to hospital without actually checking the problem first, so I have to - dubiously- confirm her rectum has actually prolapsed before we go anywhere, just in case it hasn't. I take a look, and to my surprise everything looks intact - apart from the fact she's bent over so far I can see the entirety of her vagina. I'll admit, I haven't seen hundreds of prolapsed rectums in the past though, so just to be sure I'm not missing anything, I ask my well experienced ECA to take a look. I think she thinks I'm joking at first by the look on her face. It's only when I look up with a serious expression, I'm met with her blank appearance as the penny drops. She isn't finding the situation quite so humorous now.

So here we are, two medically trained professionals staring at this young woman's unkempt anus and vagina, intently trying to depict any abnormality. We see nothing unusual, other than the fact the area doesn't seem to have come into contact with a razor for years, but that certainly doesn't require a doctor (debatable).

"Well it all looks normal to me" I assure them.

"What's that there then?" The patient's boyfriend asks in a concerned tone, whilst pointing at her labia. I pause for a second...

"Umm... well, that's her vagina" I say blankly, unsure if he's taking the piss.

"I've never seen it look like that before!"

"Have you ever seen your girlfriend bent over the couch in that position before?"

"Oh no, I guess not."

CHAPTER EIGHTEEN:

Self Castration

Working as a mixed sex crew works swimmingly sometimes. I do the ECGs on women, whilst my colleague does the attempted self castration jobs. You know, those routine jobs we go to all the time! As the job comes in and we start reading the screen, we both go completely silent before grimacing at exactly the same time.

"You're kidding me," my colleague asks rhetorically.

"Hmm, I don't think they are" I reply whilst staring at the screen, wishing and praying the words miraculously disappear. "I think you should attend this one you know, to save what dignity he has left and all"

"I agree" replies my colleague, swallowing loudly and turning a pale shade of grey.

As we enter the property, there sat on the bed is our uninterested, completely unphased patient, stark naked, holding his bloody exposed penis. He seems more pre-occupied in his telly than he does in his mangled genitals.

"I guess I'll still attend as planned then" says my colleague as he raises his eyebrows and makes his way towards the patient. "We need to stop that bleeding fella"

"Shhhh, I'm trying to watch this new game show"

"I know bud, but let us just have a little look at those wounds first shall we? We can't leave you like this

"Will you just shut up and piss off out of my house!" the patient shouts.

It's evident this elderly confused gentleman who lives in assisted living has some form of mental health disorder, just by reading the instructions written on post it notes on most of the appliances surrounding his house. This in addition to his 'did not attend' letters from the NHS mental health team piling up in the corner of the room. Judging by his age and the type of living accommodation, I'd put my money on dementia, a cruel disease. I can't quite understand how he's even got himself into this situation. Surely somebody this late on in their illness should not be living alone? Even in assisted living. Sadly for him -but I think best for everyone else- I would not be surprised if he doesn't return home following this incident, and is admitted into a nursing home, or at the very least, a care home.

My crew mate who previously worked in a psychiatric hospital is doing a fantastic job. Our patient is now passionately reminiscing about the war as if it were yesterday, whilst my ECA temporarily dresses his wounds to prevent any further blood loss. He doesn't even seem to notice that he has stopped bleeding, he's so engrossed in conversation. Before leaving for hospital I joke that the two of them are like old long lost school friends. The patient smiles at that comment.

CHAPTER NINTEEN:
STEMI

After seeing a patient with sunburn after laying on a sun bed for too long, but then refusing our help because she's finally got comfortable and doesn't want to move, we are sent to the walk in centre for a patient who has had chest pain for two days. On arrival he is obviously breathless and pale, but the GP and wife state he's been this way for forty eight hours. Despite the chest pain, the GP has been unable to perform an ECG as the walk in centre isn't equipped with one, but she informs me of her suspicions. Forty eight hours earlier the patient had begun feasting on a full English breakfast, when he suddenly noticed central crushing pain in his chest, radiating into his left shoulder and arm. His wife immediately noticed him become pale, cold and clammy and went to dial 999, but her husband refused, stating he'd sleep it off. When the pain still hadn't subsided two days later though, he finally gave in to his concerned wife, and agreed to attend his local walk in centre.

We all agree this sounds very much like a cardiac event, but I reiterate the GP, when I reassure the patient it's probably not a heart attack, as he would simply be unlikely to survive two days without treatment. That being said, there are of course plenty of other dangerous cardiac events -and non-cardiac events- which could display similar symptoms, so hospital is still by far the safest option, even if the ECG comes back perfectly normal. Reluctantly, the patient agrees. Moreover, some myocardial infarctions (heart attacks) aren't detected at all on ECGs and require a blood test for a diagnosis.

As we walk out to the ambulance the patient becomes increasingly short of breath, as if he's just sprinted the hundred meters, so we re-evaluate and bring the stretcher out to him. Coincidently, he's the only patient today to not have a respiratory rate of fourteen. By the time we reach the ambulance his heart rate has returned to a normal rate, albeit the higher end of normal. We attach an ECG quickly to assess his cardiac rhythm, and potentially the cause of the chest pain. When the ECG loads, I cannot believe my eyes, he's having a stonking inferior STEMI in his right ventricle*. A STEMI is a myocardial infarction causing ST elevation between the S and T segments on an ECG. It takes a lifetime to fully understand ECGs. We can identify which artery –or at least the approximate area of the heart - is occluded by identifying where the elevated ST segments are located. His Q waves are also extraordinarily depressed, which is a sign of irreversible necrosis. Once myocardial cells have died, nothing will restore them. Treatment will only prevent further cells from going down the same necrotic path. This is why speed is absolutely paramount. It's a weekend, so our nearest open PPCI is almost an hour away. Our local PPCI is only open Monday to Friday nine to five. You're only allowed to have a heart attack during office hours apparently.

Our patient has already waited forty eight hours, so in all honesty I'm sure he can wait another hour. When I ring up coronary care unit (CCU) to pre-alert them of the situation and gather whether we're bringing our patient straight up to PPCI or not - seeing as he's been having an STEMI for two days now - the cardiac nurse is just as unsure as I am, so informs me she'll get back to me as soon as she has had a word with the consultant. This is a very unique situation many of us have never met before, so whilst awaiting the consultant's decision, we make our way to the hospital on blues, and administer the patient a concoction of medications. One to reduce the pain and one to prevent vomiting -partly because of the morphine and partly due to travelling backwards in an ambulance travelling on blue lights. Then two to dilate the blood vessels and prevent further coagulation (clots). This should facilitate greater blood flow to and from the heart. When we arrive at the hospital, I still haven't heard back from CCU, so we have no idea where we're taking our time critical patient. Thankfully though, when we walk into ED which just so happens to be on route to CCU, we are met by a cardiac nurse, and are informed to take the patient straight into resus. Here the patient questions whether he's going to get the stent I'd vaguely talked about earlier, and I have to answer him truthfully, that I'm really not sure yet. As numerous nurses and registrars reassess the patient and ask all the same questions we did, I watch from the corner of the room, trying to learn from them and their decisions. After fifteen minutes of waiting with still no outcome though, and jobs stacking, I impatiently decide to go straight to the consultant direct when he's finished speaking with the patient, to enquire what the next steps will be. He kindly explains that they will not be taking the patient to PPCI as the myocardial cells associated with the infarct have already become necrotic, and PPCI cannot regenerate them. Therefore, the only treatment option left is symptom management. This means the patient will be left with heart failure* for the rest of his life, chronic shortness of breath, and unstable angina*. All of which could have all been avoided had he have rung 999 when he first noticed the pain. I'd much prefer go to a chest pain and it turn out to absolutely nothing, than go to a job like this.

CHAPTER TWENTY:

I Wanted To See If It Worked

On arriving at a syncope* patient, we can't help but think to ourselves she's recovered very quickly, seeing as she's leading us to her kitchen quicker than we can keep up with.

"So, start from the beginning?" I ask as we all take a seat. Note to self - never ask a patient to start from the beginning, because they will!

"Well, five years ago… was it five? It might have been six. Well anyway, six years ago I went to my GP for a tickly cough and he told me I had a virus. He was right on that occasion, but the following year I got it again, and it went straight down to my chest, so I had to be put on antibiotics for a week. Now every winter I get this blasted chest infection"

It's currently the middle of the summer.

"Actually, the year I got that first chest infection was the very same year my beloved husband died. Oh dear, he was such a lovely man he was, oh… well anyway…"

"Wha…?" I try to interrupt, but don't get a word in edgeways.

"I had my first baby late at thirty seven, then shortly after I had a hysterectomy as the doctors said I was losing too much blood. I don't think she minded being an only child though, she got all my attention, and still does today thinking about it, ha ha."

"Sorry to interrupt, what's actually happened today?" I finally manage to fit in between one of her short pauses. Suddenly the sweet, cuddly grandma turns more into a rather frightening, stern faced mother in law.

"Excuse me?! You asked me a question, don't be so rude as to interrupt me when I'm answering it young lady" she bellows.

My ECA tries hard to keep it together, but fails miserably by laughing out loud. We listen for another fifteen minutes, but my brain is switching off now. I find myself just nodding and saying: "Yes, yes" hopefully in all the right places. It's been a long day. But then suddenly a phrase catches my attention:

"Now last week"

Ah, finally we're back in the twenty first century.

"I was told I have something wrong with my heart, shortening of the arteries or something" she continues, holding up a bottle of glyceryl trinitrate (GTN) spray. She means narrowing of the coronary arteries, also known as angina*. GTN is only to be used when breathlessness and/or chest pain present themselves. If you spray GTN under your tongue when you are not experiencing these symptoms and the coronary arteries are not dangerously narrow, the excess, unnecessary vasodilation* causes hypotension* and often syncope. Pronounced sin-copy, not sign-cope as I originally thought as a first year student reading textbooks, before I actually heard someone use the term out loud. My mentor laughed at me for about ten minutes when they heard my pronunciation, quite rightly.

This is exactly what our patient had done, causing hypotension and syncope, which resolved within a few minutes. When questioned why she administered the spray when she didn't need it, her response was:

"Well I wanted to see if it worked"

Needless to say, it worked, and she didn't need to go to hospital.

CHAPTER TWENTY ONE:
Fibro Headache

We arrive in the bariatric patient's bedroom, after being led upstairs by her concerned thirteen year old daughter - who is also her main carer - and are informed she is in writhing ten out of ten pain all over her entire body, whilst calmly talking in full sentences. Some people struggle to give their pain a number and I completely get that a hundred percent, so I explain the pain score system to her further.

"Ok, so ten out of ten is the worst pain that you could ever imagine, its breaking all your bones in your body, or childbirth, or being mauled by a crocodile, you'd be unable to talk to me you'd be in so much pain. Your vital signs like your heart rate and respiration rate would be elevated and you'd be sweating profusely (which she isn't) so are you sure it's ten out of ten?"

"Yes it is" she calmly replies, with a pulse of sixty. "I'm just good at managing my pain".

Everybody experiences pain differently, and if she says she's in ten out of ten pain, who am I to disagree? I'm not in her body, so that's what I put as her pain score on my paperwork

"I understand," I reply "where exactly is the pain?"

"It's my entire body"

"Ok, well, where is it at its worst? Or where are you noticing it the most?"

"Everywhere"

"Sorry, we need you to be a little bit more specific, is it just your limbs and body, or do the soles of your feet, and your eyeballs and your teeth hurt as well?" Sounding sarcastic, but I hadn't meant it sarcastically at all.

"Yes, all of those places you mentioned, it's everywhere, it's agony"

I'm a little stumped. I've never met this situation before, and it's like getting blood out of a stone asking what kind of pain she's in, when it started and what she'd like us to do about it.

"Would you like us to arrange some pain relief for you that can be left at a pharmacy for you to collect?"

"I'm already on everything!"

She's right, her medicine cabinet is like a pharmacy. An addict would have a field day if they got their hands on even half of this. Bottles and bottles of oral morphine, diazepam, naproxin and codeine, overflowing from the small bathroom shelf onto the floor. Has she been stockpiling?

"This is a lot of medication, does none of this work for you?" I ask.

"Clearly not! Please don't leave me here, I can't stand another night like this"

She's not exactly an ideal candidate for a hospital admission, but if she's already on every analgesia* known to man and still claims to be in ten out of ten pain, there's not an awful lot else that can be done for her in her own home. I consider ringing her GP, but it's a Saturday, so I begrudgingly agree that hospital is the best course of action. The one thing she hasn't got in her stockpiled bathroom cupboard is a simple box of paracetamol.

"Have you had any paracetamol at all today?"

"Are you taking the piss? It doesn't do shit" she comes back at me.

"I understand, but I can't really take you to hospital in ten out of ten pain without giving you any of our analgesia that you haven't self-administered yet, so maybe we could just try some?"

"Ok, but put it in my vein, I don't like swallowing tablets."

Is she winding me up?

Before we attempt to mobilise the twenty five stone patient, who claims she cannot walk, we get a line in, but this seems to cause just as much pain as her original complaint.

"I just feel pain more than everybody else, it's my fibromyalgia" she confesses.

But just then, as I flush the cannula with nothing more than salty water:

"Oh my God, that's amazing, the pain is halved already. Paracetamol has never worked for me before… In fact I think the pain has gone. Thank you so much, I could cry"

"The pain has gone?" I ask.

"Yes it's gone" she replies now crying. "I don't think I need hospital after all, oh my God, I can't thank you enough"

Watching her now walk to the bathroom weeping as if Jesus has just performed a miracle, I agree she does not need to attend hospital at all. So I take the cannula out of her arm and decide how I'm going to tell her it was just salty water.

"Are you shitting me?!" She retorts, when I explain the situation honestly.

"I expect all the medications you have been taking for your pain have all finally been absorbed by your body, and that's what reduced the pain."

"No! I don't believe you. You gave me something! And whatever it is, it's helped me, so thank you. I have no intention of coming to hospital with you now though!"

Despite complete honesty, she still doesn't believe it was simple salty water I flushed into her vein, so I ask once more if she wants to attend hospital -she doesn't-, wish her well, and document my very specific and honest paperwork.

"I just hope I don't get a fibro headache after all this, sometimes I get them" she comments on our way out the door.

"A fibro headache?"

"Yes, it's not a normal headache, it's a fibromyalgia headache"

CHAPTER TWENTY TWO:
Drowning

I'm pretty nervous about this next job. It's come in as a drowning at a home address, and it's a priority one* back up from the RRV, so it must be serious. When we did scenarios at university on resus Annie dolls practicing for our dreaded objective structured clinical examinations (OSCEs), I'd often get given the drowning patients. I'm not sure why. I've rehearsed this scenario a hundred times but never once been to a real drowning. Will I excel because of all my practice? Or will I crumble as real life is nothing like scenarios? I thoroughly enjoyed scenarios at university, we always seemed to be given the worst possible scene. It wasn't just a drowning patient, it was a drowning child with their hysterical parent (another student acting), stopping you from what you're doing. Or it was a double amputee patient, and you only have one tourniquet. I loved the pressure and the problem solving, I almost miss it. But when it comes to a real life patient, it's a whole different ballgame. Besides, our scenarios were held in clean, wide open, well lit spaces. This is very rarely the case out on the road. As we pull up, my adrenaline is pumping. 'Come on Georgia, this is what you went to university for, this is what they taught you, now's your chance to use it and maybe save a life, don't fuck it up.' I think to myself.

We rush into the house where the RRV paramedic is waiting for us, and are immediately shocked to be knee deep in sewage water. I was expecting the patient to have fallen into her pond, or drowned in the bath, not the entire bottom floor of her house to be flooded! As we walk into the kitchen, the RRV paramedic is doing everything he can to get the patient out the water, but it's useless, she's largely overweight and unable to communicate in her hypothermic state.

I thought the drowning would be the cause of her reduced GCS, but it's not. She's very apparently FAST positive, with a left sided facial droop and no motor function in either side of her body. Moreover, she has a whopping haematoma* on the side of her head where we assume she fell and has most likely caused herself a bleed on the brain. What's more, the flooded water has been building up around her, leaving her hypothermic, but thankfully has narrowly missed her nose and mouth, due to the supine position she's been laid in. This isn't a drowning at all, it's so much worse. A drowning is fairly easy to fix, with a good outcome if treated early. A haemorrhagic stroke, which seems to have been developing for almost forty eight hours judging by when she was last seen well, coupled with hypothermia, does not present such a promising outcome. We all wonder whether the burst pipe came first or the stroke. Did she rush to fix the pipe causing her to slip on the water and bang her head, or did she collapse following a spontaneous bleed causing her to crack her head open, then the burst pipe occurring later? Either way, she's been pretty unlucky to say the least! And to be honest, the exact sequence of events isn't particularly relevant at this stage. We need to get her out of here and warm her up on route to the CT scanner, as quickly as possible. The poor RRV paramedic has been here almost fifteen minutes, feeling utterly helpless, as he couldn't move her cold body alone, nor perform many observations on her pale, frozen skin. Together we place a transfer sheet underneath her, then feel around under the freezing water for the handles, in an attempt to lift her. As we mobilise her from the ground, sewage water pours either side of the sheet, soaking now our entire bodies below our waists. We don't care about that though, we'll worry later. For now we need to give her all the hope she has left.

"Can you hear me?" I shout, "we're going to look after you, try not to worry, you're not alone anymore."

She has no way of communicating with me other than looking at me, but she looks me right in the eye as I speak to her. She's not completely unresponsive; even though her eyes are fixed to the right in what is called a horizontal gaze*. Her eye lids flicker up and down and the fear in her eyes is like nothing I've seen before. There's definitely some conscious thought left in her. Although it's heart breaking to watch, it gives us hope that she still might pull through.

Before we perform any intervention -we're very limited when it comes to strokes- we carry her straight onto the stretcher and into the warming ambulance, where the heater is on full. It's got so hot I almost feel like I might faint, but there's no time to faint. Her clothes, as well as ours, are saturated. She's never going to warm up with these on, so we cut them off quickly leaving her half naked but dry. Then we wrap her in both our heated blankets, before covering her up with sheets to save her dignity. We're supposed to warm her up slowly so that her body doesn't go into shock, but there's no chance of that just yet. Her temperature still reads dangerously low, not increasing from when the RRV paramedic first arrived. Unbelievably despite being bradycardic* her blood pressure remains stable – although on the lowest side of stable. So when none of us can get a cannula in her peripherally shut down body, we're not overly concerned. It seems to take an awful lot to get any paramedic even moderately concerned.

With her dried and wrapped up in the heated blankets, receiving a small but necessary amount of oxygen, we have reached our very limited skill set for a stroke. The only thing we can give her now is diesel, to get her to the CT scanner and the consultants who can help her, as quickly as is humanly possible. We leave the RRV on the scene and all travel in the ambulance, to give her the best possible chance of survival if she deteriorates. My ECA drives phenomenally. As we reach the hospital in less than ten minutes, we feel like regurgitating our breakfasts, but speed is exactly what our patient requires. Thankfully the patient doesn't deteriorate on route, and her temperature begins to increase, so we wheel her straight to CT where a team of highly skilled medics await our arrival. The RRV paramedic then commences the almost unbelievable clinical handover.

"Patient in her late fifties" we can't be more specific as the only other person to know she's here is her next door neighbour, and he doesn't know her exact age "was last seen well approximately forty eight hours ago, which is unusual for her, as she is normally seen out and about daily. At 07:00 this morning, her neighbour noticed water pouring from underneath her front door, so knocked the door down to find her lying in freezing sewage water, up to her chin coming from a burst pipe. On our arrival, we noticed the patient had a large, open but dried haematoma to the temporal region of her skull and was FAST positive, with left sided facial droop, a horizontal gaze, and no muscle tone or motor ability peripherally. The water narrowly missed her nose and mouth, making aspiration* unlikely, but it has left her hypothermic, with the thermometer reading 'low' -below 34.0. She's been GCS six throughout, and we've been unable to cannulate as she is peripherally shut down, and we didn't want to delay hospital transfer time."

The stroke team politely listen to us in silence, jaws dropped and vague expressions on some of their faces. You couldn't make this up if you tried. As the patient is wheeled into the CT scanner, we all crowd around the computer screen in anticipation. She's had a sub-dural haemorrhage*. It displays on the screen as a semicircle within the cranium, forcing the brain matter to one side. If the brain is forced unilaterally by five millimetres or more -which it is- this calls for immediate extrication of the haematoma that's compressing the brain. I wasn't initially sure if they'd perform surgery on our patient, as she has no apparent onset time, however the consultant soon informs us she'll be transferred to a major trauma centre, where the haematoma will be removed, and the pressure on her brain relieved. I'm thrilled to hear this news. Every bleed on the brain I've witnessed previously has been made comfortable, as they're outside of the window for treatment; have a DNR*; or their brain tissue is beyond repair, so I'm quite excited to hear she's having emergency brain surgery. A sub-dural haemorrhage makes perfect sense, as it can often take forty eight hours to fully develop, due to it being a venous bleed as opposed to arterial. A sub acute sub-dural haemorrhage can even take up to two weeks to fully develop.

One of the main let downs of being a paramedic is we don't always get to see the overall outcome for our patients. Now our patient is being transferred to another hospital, we will likely never know whether she survived surgery or not. The only way we will ever find out is if we are called to her again, but I doubt that will be the same address judging by the condition her house was left in. Sometimes though, I prefer not to know. If I found out she went through all that then didn't survive until discharge, I'd be absolutely gutted. In not knowing, I still have that glimmer of hope that she might have pulled through.

CHAPTER TWENTY THREE:

Stroke At The Wheel

I think my local hospital have lost all faith in me since bringing in my last male patient, who I was certain was having a per vaginal (PV) bleed.

"A PV bleed?" the nurse questioned.

"Yes a PV bleed, it started about an hour ago"

"HIS PV bleed started about an hour ago?"

"Yes" I reply, confused why he's questioning me.

"I think you mean a per rectal (PR)* bleed?" He smirks, unable to keep a laugh in any longer.

"Oh my God! Yes definitely a PR bleed. I'm so sorry"

Luckily the nurse in charge sees the funny side, and I don't think the patient is any the wiser. Let's hope I do better with my next job of the night, which comes in as a Road traffic Collision (RTC). As we pull up on scene, my ECA's Hi-Viz jacket and helmet go on quickly as we get out the cab and make our way to the involved car. He hasn't been to an RTC prior to this, which is immediately evident when he rushes up to the slightly dented vehicle all guns blazing, to find no patient. Just like I would have in my first few months in the job!

"Where is she?" He shouts.

"She's in there having a coffee" a bystander informs us, pointing to her bungalow with a confused expression on her face. Maybe this isn't as serious as we first thought.

"She's abnormally confused though" continues the neighbour. Or maybe it is.

On entering the property, we are met by a FAST positive, agitated elderly lady, in her mid eighties, highly confused why she doesn't recognise the décor in her bungalow.

"I didn't fit this kitchen, this isn't my kitchen, where am I? Where have you people taken me?" she squeals.

"It's ok, it's ok," I reassure her "you're right, this isn't your house, it's your neighbour's, she brought you in here after you crashed your car."

"Crashed my car? What are you talking about?" She cries, pushing us out the way and wobbling into her neighbour's laundry cupboard.

"I think what's probably happened is your friend has hit her head quite hard when she collided with your wall" I tell the neighbour honestly, "and it looks like she might be quite seriously ill from it, so it's important we get her to hospital as quickly as we can, would you like to come with us?"

"No, you don't understand" says the neighbour. "I watched her, she staggered into her car dizzy, after standing on her front lawn for over ten minutes staring into the darkness, then she was all over the place in the road when she started driving. I watched her hit my wall. She wasn't travelling at speed and I didn't see her hit her head. I don't think she should have been driving in the first place."

I thank the neighbour, this is really important information, very relevant to the patient's history and ongoing treatment. It would appear she had a spontaneous stroke prior to the crash. Gently, myself, my ECA and the neighbour walk our restless patient out to the ambulance where she reluctantly lays down on the stretcher. The neighbour decides to remain at home, as she informs us they aren't very close; in fact this is the first time they've actually spoken.

Our patient is talking in full sentences, but the words and phrases she's using are disjointed, making very little sense. She's also very uncoordinated on her feet, and states she feels extremely nauseous, all pointing towards a cerebellar stroke. But these are only my suspicions. Only the skilled stroke team at the hospital and a CT of her brain will confirm this.

Just as we set off to leave and I go to make a phone call to the hospital to provide a pre-alert, a loud knocking on the ambulance door brings us to an immediate halt.

"Can I help you?" I ask the elderly gentleman stood in the road.

"Can you tell me what's going on? I mean does she really need to go to hospital? She's the leader of our church choir and we really can't do without her for our show tonight. She didn't show up this evening, so I've come to get her"

"Unfortunately she's quite poorly and she certainly won't be coming to the choir tonight I'm afraid, sorry, we really have to get her to hospital now" I quickly inform the gentleman whilst trying to shut the ambulance door.

"Can I come in and talk to her? What's wrong with her? Surely it can't be bad enough to not attend the choir!" he continues, trying to barge past me and get onto the ambulance.

"Look feller! She's having a bloody stroke, now back off and let us get her to hospital before it's too late!" Is what I so badly want to say.

"We really need to leave now" is what I actually tell the non family member, as I shut the heavy side door and tell the ECA to get going before we get another knock on the door.

Finally, I commence my pre-alert over the phone, so the hospital can expect our time critical patient. Although I mention she's been involved in an RTC, all further information I provide, only includes the stroke. I think they agree it could be a cerebellar stroke, and they will have a team ready and waiting for her in resus. I don't expect this to be a full trauma team however. As we walk through the double doors into the resus department, we are met with the world and his wife! On one side of the hospital bed is the stroke team and on the other side is the full trauma team, including an anaesthetist. They are separated by one of the scariest consultants in the entire hospital. She dislikes most paramedics (or maybe it's just me she dislikes) and puts in datix's* here, there and everywhere. I'm yet to receive one as of yet, but looking at the expression on her face when I walk towards her, that's about to change.

"Oh my God, she hasn't even immobilised her!" Accuses the consultant in a loud voice, as if I'm not in the room. The nurse I handed over to earlier regarding the PR bleed is now stood in the corner of the room with his head in his hands. I'm so frustrated she's made all these clinicians doubt me without receiving any piece of information about the RTC itself, so I commence my handover before we even get the patient ready for a transfer onto the hospital bed.

"We were called to this eighty six year old lady, who was seen stumbling into her car following a ten minute vacant episode on her lawn. She barely left her driveway, travelling at no more than five mph when she drove straight into her neighbour's wall. This was witnessed and no injuries from the RTC were identified. For this reason we didn't immobilise her" I defend myself, looking directly at the consultant now.

"You can leave now" she tells the entire ten man trauma team.

Although I was frustrated she spoke about me as if I wasn't in the room, she wasn't wrong in making her point. But then she is a consultant that's spent at least ten years working her way up to her expert level, while I am - whether I like it or not - merely just another paramedic. There are tens of thousands of us, and I know really, she can talk to me however she feels fit. I damn right should have mentioned the RTC in further detail. Instead I gave them the impression a patient had been involved in some mass casualty high speed RTC and was now experiencing stroke symptoms, and that wasn't the case at all. I messed up.

Tomorrow is another day. It would just be really, really nice if nobody needs to go to hospital tomorrow, I could do with a day to consolidate... It was a cerebellar haemorrhagic stroke though.

CHAPTER TWENTY FOUR:

Cruel To Be Kind

Some jobs are just damn right heart breaking. As we pull up to our next patient's house, we are surprised to see the police already on the scene. This job came in as an elderly woman with a head injury. Has she been assaulted? I really hope not, who would do such a thing to a frail, helpless being, who had survived the war!

"We weren't expecting you to be here" we laugh as the police answer the door.

"We weren't expecting you either" they reply.

What on earth is going on?

"Well, seeing as you are here, you could probably be of great use to us actually" The police admit. "A woman in her eighties has been assaulted for we hope the last time, by her husband, who suffers worsening dementia. He has no recollection of the events and appears very calm and collected at present, but his wife claims he has spontaneous episodes of violence, before returning to his usual calm self. This time he's caused her a serious head injury, so she has reluctantly decided to seek some support. We can't take him to the station due to his dementia diagnosis and him not presenting as a threat as this present time, but we feel his wife is no longer safe here, living with him alone." The police confess.

Wow, this really is a difficult situation. There is no easy answer, so together we all congregate in the living room where the patient and his wife anxiously wait, and we commence a lengthy, difficult conversation. The wife has a haematoma and mild laceration to her forehead, but seeing as she is not anticoagulated*, did not lose consciousness and does not wish to attend hospital under any circumstances anyway, we cannot admit her to ED. If she did come to hospital with us, that would at the very least, be a temporary fix, as it gets her away from her unintentionally abusive husband, and emergency support can be arranged whilst she's gone, but she makes it very clear to us this is not an option.

"Do you know why we're here?" We question the husband.

"I expect I've been a naughty boy!" He chuckles in a deep, loving Grandpa voice.

He's a slightly overweight, adorable looking elderly gentleman, who gives the impression he'd bake cakes and do the gardening all day, with his beloved grandchildren. He has a huge smile on his face throughout the entirety of the conversation, blissfully unaware of the heartbreaking situation he's in, whilst he dips his digestives in his hot cup of tea contently.

"And why do you think you've been a 'naughty boy' then?" One of the police officers questions.

"Well I really have no idea" he laughs out loud. "But you don't have all these policemen in your house for no good reason now do you? Was I driving my bike too fast again officer? I know I shouldn't, really, it's just it's a Harley, and it's so hard to keep track of my speed."

"He hasn't had that bike in over twenty years" the wife whispers, her eyes welling up. "He really doesn't have a clue".

I feel for her greatly, but I'm still trying to work out the options for this family. The police are right, this man does not belong in a police cell, he has lost his mental capacity. I could find out whether a local star bed is available for him, but these are usually for the carers of dementia patients, and besides, they are few and far between to say the least. He would likely not get one in his local village tonight, and therefore would have to travel miles and miles, which is certainly not an appropriate treatment option for a confused dementia patient. Alternatively, I could take him to hospital as an appropriate place of safety, but again, this is not ideal. Unfortunately though, it's 22:00 on a weekend, and all other services are currently unobtainable. Social services can be made aware and we can start an emergency referral, but that would still take the rest of the night, and we would have to leave the patient and his wife here alone.

I rack my brain, but I really don't think we have any further options available at this time of the night, other than taking the patient to hospital. I'm certainly not prepared to leave them alone this evening, where he could potentially murder her through diminished responsibility. Therefore, we explain our plan to the couple and I begin an emergency social services referral, in the hope they will have something set up ready for his discharge.

"Ok, you can take him" His wife agrees reluctantly, whilst trying to hold back her tears, "but I want him back, this is just temporary!"

We all stay silent, we can't promise anything unfortunately.

"Maybe this is best" she continues, weeping now. "He'll get the support he needs and in the meantime, I can learn how to deal with his outbursts. Yes, before we know it we'll be fine, he'll learn to get better and I'll learn to control his temper." She says more cheerfully now, wiping away her tears.

How can I possibly tell her he's never going to get better and she's never going to be able to control his temper for him, as dementia is a progressive, cruel disease of the mind that will take your loved ones long before you plan their funeral? None of us have the heart, so we simply praise the wife for thinking so positively.

"Shall we get you to hospital then sir?"

"Why on earth do I need to go to hospital?"

"Just for a check up"

We can't tell him the real reason for his admission. That would be like telling somebody with paranoid schizophrenia that their hallucinations aren't real, and that's not our job. They believe their delusions and hallucinations just as they believe the sky is blue. If somebody told you that you don't have three children (when you do), or that you are not a woman, you're a man (or vice versa), it's all just a delusion, you'd say don't be so stupid, of course I have three children, or I am a man/woman. That's exactly what it's like for psychotic patients when they are told it's all in their heads. I've heard doctors refer to dementia and schizophrenia as on par with cancer.

"Well I trust you people with my life, so if you really think I need to go, then I suppose I better," he consents. It's tear jerking.

In all honesty I don't know what will happen from here, but I have a suspicion he will never come home to his wife again. Now his dementia is causing violence to himself and his relatives, I expect he will be admitted to a nursing home. It's horrific, but sometimes you have to be cruel to be kind, eventually he could kill his wife and have no idea what he's done.

CHAPTER TWENTY FIVE:
Septic Shock

We've been sent to the dreaded walk in centre that doesn't have an ECG again, and what do you know? It's for another chest pain. My crew mate knows the GP who's leading us towards the consultation room well, where the patient awaits.

"How did your ultra marathon go?" He asks her.

Ultra marathon? It's just not fair, as well as being beautiful and a talented GP, she can also run ultra marathons. I try to remember jealousy is a sin, but then remember I'm not at all religious, so carry on feeling exactly the way I choose to.

The GP introduces us to the patient.

"This morning she awoke with chest tightness and rigors*. She's been increasingly lethargic for five days, has had an intermittent fever and a productive cough. This morning she felt too weak to get out of bed or fully open her eyes, so her concerned husband carried her into his car and drove her here."

It's immediately apparent this patient is septic. Her hands are like ice, whilst her skin is as pale as a sheet, except for her cheeks which are flushed in colour. She's profusely diaphoretic*and is struggling to stay awake in the plastic chair. What's more, the GP has had to stop and restart her sentence multiple times between the patient's chesty, brutal coughing episodes.

"It's so painful" she cries between breaths. "Every cough is like being stabbed in the chest." Unfortunately she has left it so long to see a GP, her intercostals muscles that allow her chest to expand, have become painfully sore and inflamed, so she's also got costachondritis,* as well as sepsis. I remember the name of this condition by telling myself costa-coffee-itis, just as I remember Clopidogrel* by saying cloppy-dog-roll.

Her abnormal vital signs put together add up to a NEWS2 score of eleven. She is definitely a patient for a blue light transfer, straight to resus. People die of sepsis every day, this is a medical emergency. These patients often compensate so well for so long, then all of a sudden go into multi-organ failure and begin breathing ineffectively, or become unconscious as a result of hypotension and septic shock*.

I've been to so many other walk in centres and GP surgeries hundreds of times and not had a singular time critical patient there yet, I'm convinced this walk in centre is cursed. As we wheel our patient out through the main and only entrance, on oxygen and with a saline drip underway, the busy waiting room suddenly turns silent and all eyes are fixed on us. I wonder if they're just curious or if they're panicked that they might catch something.

As I read out my pre-alert to the receiving hospital I can't quite believe the severity of my patients condition myself, every possible vital sign that could be deranged is. I've been to many septic patients but none have been this time critical. Blood pressure, oxygen saturations, heart rate, respiration rate, temperature and blood glucose, all far from within their normal parameters. Her NEWS2 has gone up to fourteen now. Thankfully we're only about ten minutes from our local resus, where they can start her on an emergency IV antibiotic drip, and correct her deranged blood gases. All we can do is raise her blood pressure by forcing salty water into her vein, administer IV paracetamol, and provide her with hypoxic lungs with oxygen. We can't administer morphine as this would drop her already dangerously low blood pressure. It'll do temporarily but it won't save her life. We like to think of ourselves as highly skilled specialist clinicians, underpaid doctors to some degree, but I've learnt to never underestimate what it really takes to be a doctor. Regular paramedics on the road most days are just glorified taxi drivers, driving to the big white building where the real intervention starts. It's only on the very rare occasion we go to a hypoglycaemic*, or asthmatic patient, or a cardiac arrest that our skills and autonomy really come into play. Even at RTCs, we mostly just stabilise the patient for their journey to hospital, then let the real adults get to work. Don't get me wrong, the ever changing developing role of paramedics means there are so many other avenues and opportunities available. For example, I know of more than one specialist paramedic (SP) that has gone on to complete their advanced practitioner and prescribing courses within a hospital setting, where once qualified, they are the equivalent of an F1 doctor*. Plus, more and more paramedics are going into urgent and primary care nowadays, assessing and diagnosing their own patients in a GP consultation room Monday to Friday nine until five. In one respect that is not why I became a paramedic, I want to be out there on the front line, making a positive difference to patients in their own homes, going through potentially the worst part of their lives. I feel privileged to be allowed into people's homes and lives during their time of need. Besides I'm not done seeing the serious, sometimes gruesome jobs, and feeling the adrenaline pumping around my body when I save a life, or get a return of spontaneous circulation (ROSC) after a cardiac arrest. But on the other hand, we are very rarely diagnosing professionals. Sure, we identify STEMIs and UTIs, but we're not the ones treating our patient with antibiotics or booking the patient into theatre to undergo coronary intervention. That's specialist paramedics (SPs) and doctors. I would absolutely love to get my masters degree and prescribing course, and start diagnosing my own urgent patients. For these reasons I choose to do it all! One day, I will get my masters and my prescribing, doing bank shifts in GP surgeries, minor injury units (MIUs) and urgent care centres, whilst working part time on the front line ambulance. At least that's the long term goal.

As we wheel our septic patient into resus, we are met by what looks like the entirety of the emergency department. I couldn't be more relieved, as our patients GCS has reduced substantially. Her eyes are closed, she is no longer communicating with us, other than squeezing my hand when I ask her to, and her breathing has become laboured. I honestly think if we got here even ten minutes later her breathing would have become ineffective. As soon as I finish my handover, trying to sound as calm as possible whist the patient looks like she might die in front of me, staff rush from pillar to post, drawing up antibiotics, getting a ventilator set up, and cannulating her opposite arm with the largest needle they can find. She's now completely unresponsive and will very soon require intubating, I imagine. Despite reading it in textbooks a hundred times, I'm surprised to see how quickly she's deteriorated. I can only hope we got her here quick enough.

I'm not ready to quit this emergency side of the job yet... I've barely just begun!

CHAPTER TWENTY SIX:

My last day as a student

I remember the job like it was yesterday, it was my final day as a student before qualifying as a paramedic. I had joked to my mentor who was feeling particularly nauseous after eating all the dark Lindt chocolate I had bought him as a thank you gift for putting up with me for my final year in training, that I would love a 'proper job' before they let me loose with my own patients. And my stupid wish was immediately granted.

Whilst my mentor pulled up to the famous landmark for the traumatic cardiac arrest, only minutes in front of another two ambulances who had been allocated the call, I enthusiastically swung the side door open before the vehicle had even come to a complete halt, and I rushed towards the manic scene. The crowds were ridiculous, hundreds and hundreds of bodies gravitating towards the scene on the glorious summer's day. I quickly overtook all the bystanders in a nervous but excited manner with the very heavy resuscitation kit in tow, followed by my mentor and ECA. I felt like we were walking for miles between the tourists in the overpowering sun, but it can't have been any more than twenty metres. When we do eventually reach the patient, who is hidden very successfully by a makeshift curtain to keep bystanders away, we witness an enthusiastic gentleman, who must be near retirement, performing CPR on the still, lifeless body. What's more, the patient has already been defibrillated twice. The public often completely forget about the defibrillator, and perform solely CPR until help arrives. Which is still fantastic by the way.

"Well done sir, you're doing an amazing job there, can we just recheck the patient for a pulse" we ask. He willingly comes straight off the patient's chest with a sigh of relief and sweat pouring off his bushy eyebrows.

"Of course, sorry, sorry."

"He has a pulse" I exclaim "Don't apologise, you might have just saved this man's life" I laugh whilst giving him a pat on the back.

Despite having a pulse, he wasn't out of the woods yet though, he could have re-arrested just as easily as his heart had restarted, so we quickly proceeded with our post ROSC care*. By that point, we were surrounded by two more ambulance crews, making it seven clinicians on scene, excluding helicopter emergency medical service (HEMS), who were preparing to land above our head. I hadn't worked with HEMS before in my entire three years of training, so to say I was excited was a huge understatement.

Having this many paramedics, ECAs and students was fantastic, we all had our own individual roles. I had just got my kit ready to cannulate, so I carried on with that in one arm whilst another paramedic cannulated the opposite limb. Two clinicians ran back and forth retrieving vital equipment, whilst others temporarily patched up the full thickness open head wound on the back of the patient's skull and one dealt with crowd control, leaving the last paramedic to hand over to HEMs. It was working like clockwork.

But then all of a sudden, when I finally looked up after being so engrossed in performing my task, I noticed I was being filmed. We all were. There stood right before our eyes was a surprisingly calm lady filming the whole event whilst commentating in French. It was only when we got a translator on the phone we realised this woman was actually the patient's wife! We couldn't get our heads around it, why on earth would anyone ever want to film their dying husband? 'Here you go kids, watch this video of your Dad being electrocuted back to life and his ribs being crushed by good CPR on our holiday in England'. But when telling the ludicrous, unlikely story to HEMS, they made a very interesting and probable point. The health care is by no means free in France, so she might have needed that footage to use as proof to claim on her insurance. It all made sense, but at the time we were all shell shocked, looking at one another as if to say: This can't really be happening, can it? This is some messed up shit!

Whilst waiting the obligatory ten minutes before we transferred the patient onto the stretcher, HEMs identified the cause of the arrest. When walking back to the car, the patient became unconscious, causing him to collapse and hit his head on a large, sharp piece of wood, making the head wound a secondary injury. On performing an ECG it was evident the patient was having a cardiac event. With this piece of information coupled with good history taking from the HEMS doctor, the cause of arrest was identified as a STEMI as a result of an abdominal aortic aneurysm (triple A). The patient had been awaiting surgery for the aneurysm, but unfortunately whilst still waiting, a clot blew off from the aneurism and occluded itself in one of his coronary arteries, causing the arrest. On collapsing he then hit his head hard, causing trauma to his skull. This realisation left the HEMS doctor and paramedic in a lengthy debate about which hospital to transfer him to though, and by which means of transport. The doctor - the senior clinician - wished to transport the time critical patient to the Major Trauma Centre (MTC) by air. They could rapid sequence intubate (RSI)* him if necessary, and get him there in half the time any road ambulance could. The HEMs paramedic however, was adamant the patient should be transferred to the local hospital by road; and he just wouldn't budge on his decision. I was in utter awe to see the specialist senior clinicians at work, like they were gods or something, but the other clinicians around me quickly became impatient and frustrated.

"Look just do something will you, the more you stand around here arguing between yourselves, the less likely the patient is to survive" shouted one of the paramedics. "I don't care what you choose, just bloody damn well do it or all our hard work would be for nothing" another retorted.

He had a point, it must have looked so unprofessional to the bystanders who were watching the whole event unfold before their eyes, and he was right, if a STEMI had indeed caused the arrest, he would be highly likely to re-arrest without treatment. Eventually the critical care paramedic relented, knowing it really wasn't his clinical decision to make overall. Personally though, I thought he was very courageous to question the doctor. I would never have questioned such an experienced clinician at the time. I would have loved more than anything to travel in that helicopter with the critical care team, but unfortunately students aren't even allowed to do observational shifts with the crew, let alone assist them.

Later in the week I got a message from my mentor. 'He survived' it read. 'The patient survived the transfer to the MTC and the clot was removed almost immediately. What's more, he didn't have any lasting brain damage from his head injury'. I was overjoyed at the result, what a job to finish on before I was out there on my own!

CHAPTER TWENTY SEVEN:
Another Amitriptyline Overdose

I've been to far too many suicide attempts. Thankfully only a handful of these regular jobs succeed, but that's not to say they won't try again in the following weeks. The ones that really get to me though are the children. We're attending a fifteen year old girl today who has attempted suicide for the ninth time, this time because she broke up with her boyfriend last night. I haven't been to her before and neither has my ECA, but looking at previous paperwork, she's attempted many unsuccessful methods of suicide in the past, including a hanging, an overdose and cutting her wrists. Today she has taken another overdose, twenty of her mum's amitriptyline*. My ECA drives like the wind on a blue light response whilst I quickly calculate the toxic dose of amitriptyline, using the average weight of a fifteen year old girl. Of course we know she's had a toxic dose, but an app on my phone helps me identify how greatly she's poisoned her body, and what symptoms we can expect from this exact dose. It reads 'symptoms could include: pyrexia*, tachycardia, unconsciousness, seizures and/or cardiac arrest'. I just hope we get there in time.

The patients mum who appears extremely calm to begin with, leads us to the troubled fifteen year old girl, who is laid down in bed with her eyes open. Her eyes are red raw from continual crying, and there is a bowl of vomit next to her bed. I'm so relieved to see she's still conscious, even if she does tell me to piss off.

"We're here to help you love" says my ECA, as he crouches down next to her. He's absolutely fantastic with these patients, as his previous line of work was in a psychiatric hospital for twenty years! If I was going to have any ECA with me today, I want this one.

"I don't want your help!" she retorts.

"Ok, I understand. I know it must be really frustrating having us come into your home and try telling you what to do at fifteen, but it's really critical you come to hospital with us before you deteriorate" continues the ECA

"NO! Go away!"

"Yes! Come on, get out of bed and go with these people to the hospital please" the patients mum interrupts, clapping her hands twice, as if saying 'you're late for school, come on, get up.'

It makes sense why the teenagers mum is so calm, not only has she been in this exact situation eight times before, she is also a registered nurse. Her relaxed demeanour quickly changes though.

All the patient's observations are miraculously stable, so we stand her up -reluctantly on her part- and walk her to the ambulance. Just as she stands though, thrashing her arms out telling us:

"I can stand alone thank you!" Her body becomes limp and she collapses to the ground hard, before having a tonic clonic seizure. She immediately bites her tongue, causing blood to pool in her oropharynx (upper airway) and is urinarily incontinent. This is all too much for her mother. She breaks down, collapsing to a crouched position next to her daughter, screaming into her chest. In some respects, you'd expect a nurse to be more calm in this situation, she must have seen seizures a thousand times during her time on ICU, but realistically this is her daughter, her flesh and blood, and I'll be the first to admit all medical knowledge goes straight out the window when you're dealing with someone you love.

"It's ok, it's ok, this is a very typical reaction to the drug she's overdosed on, we're just going to pop an oxygen mask around her nose and mouth and my ECA is going to get the stretcher from the ambulance, ok?"

Quickly the seizure subsides, and the patient slowly opens her eyes, confused and drowsy. This time we use the carry chair to get her to the stretcher, as opposed to allowing her walk.

"I'm so sorry, you must think I'm an awful nurse and mum. I was being stupid, I'm so sorry, it's just I've never seen her have such a bad reaction to an overdose before."

"Don't be silly, we don't think that of you at all! You have seen seizures so you know the negative impact they can have on the patient, and this is your daughter. I've reacted exactly the same when a member of my family is in an emergency" admits my colleague, and he's so right.

On route to resus I have a lengthy conversation with the patient's mum about her daughter's mental health, whilst she remains oblivious and confused on the stretcher following her seizure. Fortunately she doesn't seize again, so no drugs need to be administered into the vein we cannulated earlier.

"Has she been receiving much support from the child and adolescent mental health service (CAMHS)?" I ask.

"Nothing! We've been to and from the GP, but the funding has been cut, so all she gets is a weekly chat with her under qualified school counsellor, which excuse my language, is a load of bollox!"

"Nothing from the NHS?" I ask.

"Nope, literally nothing, she was under CAMHS, but like I say they've cut the funding so she's been discharged. The thing is, they say every suicide attempt has been half hearted, so say she's likely just doing it for attention. She's never taken this many pills before, but I knew she would eventually. I warned them, and they wouldn't listen to me. I know my daughter better than anyone, and now look where we are!"

"Yes you do. I just hope for you both that this is a turning point and they finally start listening." I really mean this, but I'm not holding my breath after what I've already heard and have gathered from previous patients.

I absolutely hate attending these jobs, and I couldn't get my head around why that was, for a long time. These patients are just as deserving of our service as any physically ill patient. But then one day I realised, there is literally nothing I can do to help, and that's my job, helping people. I'm so used to attending patients and fixing them before moving on to my next patient to be fixed, but I can't cure a mental health patient, at least not overnight. It takes months and months of treatment and recovery, which I will never be a part of as a paramedic.

CHAPTER TWENTY EIGHT:
Working Relationship

I'm working with 'A' and his third year student today. We're not really supposed to work together, even now that I'm qualified, for obvious reasons, but seeing as I'm doing overtime at 'A's station, my ECA has called in sick last minute, and 'A' is on the car with his student, it makes perfect sense for management to crew us up together. It's nice in a way because we get to finish at the same time for a change and we're almost a three manned paramedic crew with me, 'A' and his third year, nearly qualified student.

Due to the fact I wanted to spend as much time with 'A' as possible (he's actually the best paramedic and mentor I know, and I learnt most of what I know today from him), I continuously asked to come out on shifts with him as often as possible, between our weekly climbing sessions. To which he obliged. It wasn't until I was in my second year with a new mentor though, six months later, I finally told him how much I liked him. No more hints. After another fantastic climbing session with him and his regular ECA, the road back to his just so happened to be blocked, so we took a diversion, adding over an hour to our journey. When we arrived at his gone 23:00, we all decided to stay and eat pizza, watch climbing videos and get drunk, at which point I told him how much I really liked him. Unfortunately though, I fell unconscious in a drunken mess immediately after revealing this information, and I woke up very disappointed alone and fully clothed in his bed the next morning. He had slept in his sleeping bag on the sofa after carrying my drunken, lifeless body to bed. Two weeks later however we were an item, and I couldn't believe my luck.

"We'll have to tell the university so they don't assign you as my mentor again" I told him in bed one day.

"I have already emailed them a few months ago as I thought this might happen, and even if it didn't, I couldn't have a student that I was attracted to" he replied, to my surprise.

For our first job of the morning we are sent to a patient who's pale and clammy. Although these symptoms can be a medical emergency depending on the reasoning behind them, I don't read anymore into the job other than what is says on the screen, as nine times out of ten, it's never even remotely similar to what we've actually been sent to. 'A' and his student though say they have a bad feeling about this one. They can't put their finger on what exactly, but something feels inherently wrong, like a gut instinct. Driving on blues and twos to the scene immediately feels pointless though when we are left stood on the doorstep for five minutes after ringing the doorbell numerous times.

When the patient's daughter does eventually answer, we are met by a middle-aged woman with learning difficulties, informing us:

"There's something wrong with Mum."

Getting more of a history out of her than this though seems to be impossible, so we continue walking to her Mother's flat in silence.

"Here she is." The daughter points at her unresponsive mother.

"Oh my God" the student comments, uttering the exact words we were all thinking.

"Get her out" 'A' retorts, regarding the daughter, whilst feeling the patients pulse.

Our patient is slumped over in her chair, GCS three, grey and cyanotic all over her half naked body. Her chest is so hyper-inflated*, it abnormally protrudes past both her chin and her abdomen. With loose empty inhalers around the home, it can likely only be one of two things: Asthma or COPD. Her breathing is agonal* and her pulse approximately ten beats per minute, but that's not what particularly phases me mentally. It's her glazed over, fixed open eyes, staring right through me. She's technically still alive, but looking into her eyes, she's gone, and she's been gone a long time. As we gently lye her down to ventilate her and apply the defibrillation pads, her heart stops beating, quicker than we expected. Just that brief gentle movement was too much for her, so we commence a full resus. With almost three paramedics, it's the quickest resus I've ever done. 'A' intubates perfectly and manages the airway, whilst I administer drugs and the student provides chest compressions and rhythm checks. Within minutes we get her back and so we wait the obligatory ten minutes before rushing her to hospital, while still supplying her with high flow oxygen through the endotracheal ET tube, in the back of the ambulance. I desperately want to handover in resus to impress 'A' and show him what a great paramedic I am now, but I know it's only fair to let the student do it. These opportunities are few and far between and it might well be their last time critical handover before qualifying.

As we sit in ED's staff room typing up paperwork, wondering how long our patient was sat there, terrified, struggling to breath -probably days- the ED consultant we know well from HEMS, comes in to break the bad news.

"Her blood gases are so deranged, there's no coming back from this, so we're going to make her comfortable, but well done for all your hard work"

My first ROSC* I've got since being a registered clinician, and it's been called in resus*. I still haven't brought someone back from the dead, even when I saw them die right before my eyes. I'm disappointed, but I'm mostly extremely concerned for the patient's poor daughter, who now has no mum. Or carer.

CHAPTER TWENTY NINE:
RTC

It's so important to treat every patient equally, no matter what your prejudices or beliefs. The man who bombed London Bridge deserves the same level of treatment from us as his victims, as does a drunk driver who killed a child. It's part of our job to detach and be capable of complete non-judgement, no matter how disgusting or cruel we believe the act.

We've just pulled up to a road traffic collision (RTC) on a country road where a gentleman has just been driving his brand new Porsche home from the pub, just ten minutes away from his home address. Luckily, we know he is still conscious on our arrival as we can hear him bellowing in pain, from the crumpled foot well of the wreckage, that has rolled over numerous times; and thankfully no one else has been involved in the collision. We can't call it an accident anymore just in case it wasn't an accident at all, so collision it is. It sounds like something out of a horror film, the man's screams coming from the demolished car. The car which only stopped when it came in to contact with a huge oak tree with some force. He swerved off the country lane above, causing him roll down a steep grassy hill, before coming into contact with the tree, on a minor road below.

The road he landed on is already closed on our arrival, and the fire service are on scene; who have briefed me of the situation, following a chat with the patient. With another two ambulances on their way, this patient hopefully has every chance of survival. As I make my way towards the wreckage in anticipation, I force myself not to feel anything for the patient, not rage for drink driving, or sympathy for him losing all his retirement money he put into a Porsche in a split second, nothing. I just have a job to do and that's to protect and preserve this patient's life, to the very best of my ability.

I'm surprised but relieved to not see any obvious major trauma staring me in the face, no open fractures, or blood loss or airway compromise, but that's far from meaning he's not seriously injured, so I gather key pieces of information quickly whilst performing a full primary survey* and a full set of vital signs. Selfishly, I try to fit in as much as I can alone before the other two crews arrive. I don't really know why though, being a paramedic and saving a life is never about an individual hero.

"Where's the pain?" I ask, after checking his lungs and cervical spine with no obvious deficits.

"My abdomen, just get me out of here! I'm in agony" he shrieks, tears rolling down his face.

"Were working on it I promise, I think the fire crew are getting ready to cut the roof off" I reassure.

As I pull his shirt up again to get a better look of his abdomen and back, I can't distinctly see any abnormalities, but like I say, that means nothing. He

could be haemorrhaging internally and we wouldn't know until his body stops compensating or bruising appears, which may be too late. Just as I start immobilising his neck - purely due to the mechanism of injury and potential of distracting injuries, rather than any apparent cervical spine tenderness - my manager, a specialist paramedic and two more paramedics with their ECAs crowd around the car. They're awaiting my handover.
'This is going to have to be good' I tell myself.
"Ok, so this gentleman was travelling home from the pub, when he swerved on the unlit road above, causing him to roll twice onto the road below, impacting with a tree. He has no spinal tenderness, but I have immobilised him due to the mechanism of injury. He's complaining of ten out of ten right upper quadrant abdominal pain and has a sixteen gauge cannula* in his right arm. That's as far as I've got".

"How old is he?" Questions one of my colleagues. Oh shit, I forgot to include the A in the ATMIST!*

"How old are you sir?" I ask.

"I don't see why that really matters, but I'm fifty nine!" he shouts aggressively as he winces in pain.

"And was he wearing a seatbelt?" Another clinician that I haven't met before questions.
'Ah very good point, that I also forgot to check… but I can tell you his heart rate and blood pressure and that he's not having a tension pneumothorax at

this present moment in time, if that helps?' I think to myself, while remaining silent.

Seeing as our patient's blood pressure hasn't dropped even remotely, suggesting no apparent life threatening internal haemorrhage, we all agree to administer morphine to the screaming casualty, ready for his extrication. This seems to help somewhat whilst he is sat perfectly still in the driver's seat, but as soon as the caved in roof is successfully removed and we attempt to lay him onto our stretcher, well let's just say his language is colourful. He shrieks a painful cry that couldn't be mistaken for anything else other than pure agony, so we sit him back down and establish where the pain is originating from, to check we haven't missed anything.

"It's my abdomen still, it feels like it's being ripped in two, I can't do it, please help me" he pleads.

"Of course we will, but do you have any pain in your legs or your pelvis?"

"No, none."

We have already palpated his long bones* and his pelvis with no deficits, and have removed his heavy tracksuit bottoms, leaving him in just a pair of boxers. This allows us to identify any immediate trauma, and as all appears normal we administer another dose of morphine, ready for another extrication attempt. On his second and final attempt he screams an ear deafening cry once more, but this time he manages to stay limp whilst we place him gently onto the stretcher.

When we finally get into the compact ambulance, after wheeling the stretcher through heaps of mud and car debris at the side of the road, we barely all fit. There's myself, my manager, a specialist paramedic, and another regular paramedic with their ECA. To my pleasant surprise, my manager allows me to stay, as I was first on the scene and I am the only NQP here, so he feels this is a great learning opportunity for me.

"Ok what do we need to do next?" asks my manager, probably testing me.

I look at the almost naked patient after carrying out a full primary and secondary survey -twice - and wonder what else he could possibly mean. He has two wide bore cannulas in each arm, his vital signs are being checked every two minutes and he's had the maximum dose of morphine I am authorised to administer. What am I missing? Come on Georgia, think! This is your manager testing you. I try to think, as I scan the patient up and down, but come up with nothing other than getting him to hospital. Fast.

"Anyone else?" my manager retorts. Shit, I got it wrong. My one chance to prove myself as a competent paramedic and I fuck it up! What the hell is he looking for, that I have I missed?

"FLAPS TWELVE*, we need to check for tracheal deviation, wounds, surgical emphysema…" A colleague answers.

"Oh no wait, I've done all that - twice" I interrupt. "There is no evidence of respiratory trauma".

"Ok, well that's it then, let's make a move!" The manager requests.

Oh dear! I did exactly what he expected of me, but I forgot to actually tell anyone.

Three of us travel in the ambulance with the patient whilst the ECA drives and my manager travels by car. I am accompanied by an experienced paramedic and the specialist paramedic, both highly skilled professionals, far more experienced than me, but seeing as I was first on scene, I'm expected to perform the handover in resus. I've done this many times before, and I don't seem to get nervous any more, but I've never had my manager peering over my shoulder whilst doing so in the past.

Thank goodness the handover runs rather smoothly, and I remember to include the patient's age this time, and the fact that he was indeed wearing a seatbelt. Just as I get ready to clean the kit and head back to the ambulance, the specialist paramedic who attended interrupts:

"Do you not want to see the full trauma CT?" She whispers in my ear, knowing full well I'll say yes.

"Are we allowed to do that?" I question.

"Of course, I used to work here, come with me."

As our manager and final ambulance leave, we quickly make our way to the CT scanner, where our patient is about to discover the extent of his injuries. I almost run there, I'm so excited. I've never seen a head to toe trauma CT scan before, and it will be amazing to follow this job through for a change. As the screen loads I'm mesmerised by the images, but in all honesty have absolutely no idea what I'm looking at. First, I notice a large hollow oval shape in his abdomen.

"Is that blood?" I whisper to the specialist paramedic.

"No that's his stomach, it doesn't usually look like that, but it's full of beer. That's why you feel sick and bloated after one too many pints!"

As the screen continues to scan the rest of his body, the consultant verbalises what she is writing on her computer screen:

"Laceration to the liver…"

"Oh my God, did you hear that?" I whisper to my colleague, like a kid on Christmas morning. "He's lacerated his liver, what will they do?" The specialist paramedic just chuckles at my enthusiasm.

"…Bilateral but stable pelvic fracture" the consultant continues.

Now we're both amazed! We look to each other concerned that we didn't apply a pelvic binder, seeing as we thought we excluded a pelvic injury early on in the assessment.

"A pelvic fracture?" The highly trained paramedic questions, in a more serious tone now.

"Yes, but its stable," the consultant assures us.

A stable fracture means there has been no misalignment or dislocation of the bone or joint. It has simply been sheared or chipped, but remained in its correct anatomical position. It's rare to have a bilateral fracture and the bone to remain perfectly in place, but for this lucky gentleman, it has. It is likely the pain from the liver laceration was so severe, that he didn't even notice the pain in his pelvis. His abdominal pain was a distracting injury. That is exactly why we still immobilise these patient's necks, even when they aren't complaining of bony tenderness across their spine. They may be so engrossed in their pain elsewhere that they fail to notice the additional tenderness coming from an unstable fracture in their neck. If moved in the wrong way, the broken bone fragments may well sever their spinal cord and immediately stop their heart. It's been known to happen.

When we travel back to the vehicles, which have been left at the scene so that we could all travel in the same ambulance to hospital, the specialist paramedic rings our manager and puts the phone on speaker.

"You won't believe this mate. We've just come out of the CT scanner with that patient, and they identified a BI-LATERAL(!) pelvic fracture, can you believe it??"

"What the fuck, are you serious mate? I couldn't have predicted that" a shocked, loud voice exclaims, coming from the work phone.

"I know mate! And what's more he refused a breathalyser. I wonder if he knows the police will still arrest him when the nurses provided them with a vial of his blood if he is indeed intoxicated.

Anyway better go, Georgia's just pulling up at my car."

CHAPTER THIRTY:

A Song Can Bring Back A Thousand Memories

It's funny how a singular song can bring back a thousand memories. We're doing a transfer from our local hospital to a major trauma centre, for a seventeen year old that's been involved in a road traffic collision. We've literally just finished our break and the local hospital is just around the corner, so we arrive in a matter of minutes. Perhaps too soon, as the doctors have not yet informed the patient and her family of the extent of her injuries. While lying on the back seats of her friend's car, asleep with only a lap belt around her waist, she has fractured her spine and severed her spinal cord, leaving her paralysed from the waist down. The medics have all been frantically rushing around contacting the receiving hospital and re-evaluating her x-rays, so much so, that they haven't actually got round to telling her the harrowing news yet. So whilst me and my ECA wait silently in the corner of the room, ready to transport her on an emergency blue light response, we watch as the consultant paediatrician* delicately, but honestly, informs the patient and her family that she will likely be in a wheelchair for the rest of her life. She likely won't walk again, or be able to open her bladder and bowels the conventional way, nor be intimate with her partner again. Her father is in utter shock, pale, jaw dropped, eyes welling up, he doesn't know how to react. Her boyfriend is crying loudly into her chest. But the patient herself is surprisingly calm, reacting in the same way you might when you don't get any Facebook likes on what you thought was a revolutionary post. She looks the consultant right in the eyes and calmly says:

"Oh ok, well at least I didn't die".

The consultant now looks just as shocked as the patient's father.

We very carefully transfer the teenager from the hospital bed onto our stretcher and secure her inside the ambulance. Her dad and boyfriend choose to travel separately in their cars, so they can stop at the shops to get her some necessities.

"Are you in any pain?" I ask her.

"No I don't feel a thing!" She laughs. I nervously laugh with her. Is that what I'm supposed to do in this situation?

"So anyway, what do you do? Are you still studying?"

"Yeah, I'm at college"

"Oh that's great, what do you study?"

"Sport."

That's quickly the end of that conversation. Not long after, she asks me if she can listen to some music in the ambulance. Thank goodness as I've quickly run out of things to talk about which won't sound insensitive or patronising.

"Of course" I reply.

I wrongly assume she's going to put on some dub step, or house music given her age. But instead, I'm surprised to hear *Elton John's Rocket Man* playing from her huge new phone.

"Great music taste" I tell her as I look up from my paperwork, but she just looks straight through me. "Are you ok?" I ask sympathetically.

And just like that, as the chorus plays, her world comes crumbling down on her. The realisation that she isn't going to walk again suddenly hits her all at once, and she begins sobbing. She doesn't stop for a long time, at least for the whole time we spend with her, and it's heart breaking to watch. She wasn't even the driver, her friend was driving her home from a concert they had both been to.

As we pull up to the better equipped hospital and are eventually reunited with her boyfriend and father, we watch as they all take a moment and have a painful cry together. These are the worst parts of the job. I joined the ambulance service to make a positive difference to people's lives, whether that's saving a life or making a hot cup of tea for a frail elderly patient following a fall, but here I just feel so helpless. There is literally nothing I can say or do to make this situation even remotely better. All I can do is sympathise the best I can.

For the rest of the shift I have to try hard to not become frustrated about the bullshit jobs, like the lady we're sent to, who broke her finger three days ago. She even dared to tell her boyfriend she was being rushed to the emergency department in an ambulance and tells him if he doesn't arrive immediately to comfort her, she will certainly break up with him. I see no blue flashing lights, perhaps she's in a different ambulance to me. Or the forty year old gentleman who needed coaxing to open his bowels before telling us he's managed it and we can now leave. It's nothing new though, we go to these jobs all the time and I'm usually completely fine with it, it's not the jobs this evening, it's me.

Normally I have the utmost compassion for every single one of my patients no matter the complaint, but that often means after a twelve hour shift, I have nothing left for my family. Or more like fourteen or fifteen hours after overruns. I'm all compassioned out by then. I really cannot be bothered to ring my Mum who lives three hours away and make polite conversation, or go visit my niece and nephew only around the corner. In the moment I couldn't even care less that 'A' is sat up on his own for another night, because I'm just so damn exhausted, and it's all because I've given away my every ounce of empathy to complete strangers. When I hear *Rocket Man* now, I don't think of fond childhood memories, I think of the poor young girl who was told she'll never walk again. It's so important to find a work/life balance, or it'll mess you up.

CHAPTER THIRTY ONE:

Confirmation Bias

I'm convinced we've been called to a patient with a gastroenteritis. It's early on a Monday morning, and the patient who normally lives alone is vomiting continuously, informing me:

"It's coming out both ends".

Her daughter who is currently staying with her, became concerned in the night, as her mother was unable to keep down her regular medication, so she dialled 999.

"Are you in any pain?" I ask the patient.

"Just discomfort in my abdomen and a mild headache."

I'm immediately struck by confirmation bias, which is where someone unintentionally includes all the signs and symptoms that fit their diagnosis, and excludes anything that doesn't. She's already told me it's coming out of both ends and she has abdominal pain. It's obvious, she has gastroenteritis. Her headache must be there as a result of dehydration. However, when she doesn't seem to have a high fever, or have any other signs of infection, I brush it off as irrelevant and immediately return to my original diagnosis.

From now on it didn't matter whether I asked her when the pain started, what score she'd give the pain, or if she's experienced this pain before, its gastroenteritis. I ring her GP in an attempt to get her an appointment this morning, or see if they can prescribe her an anti-sickness, so she can resume swallowing her daily medications, but they aren't open for another half hour. Therefore, when I complete my assessment and history taking, I ask the daughter if she wouldn't mind ringing the GP surgery when they open, to explain the situation and attempt to get her mum an appointment or telephone consultation. She kindly obliges, so we get ready to leave the scene, ready for our next job.

"But how am I going to get to the GP?" The patient anxiously shouts, as we are on our way out. "I'm so dizzy, I can't bear to move".

"Dizzy?" I ask. She hadn't mentioned any dizziness the entire time we've been here.

"Yes, the room is spinning, and every time I go to stand I lose my balance and feel more nauseated."

Just as I'm about to leave, alarm bells start ringing in my head, so I quickly put my kit back down in her hallway.

"Where exactly is that headache?" I ask.

"The back of my head."

"And when you say it's been coming out of both ends? Have you had diarrhoea?"

"No, I meant my waterworks, but I'm on Furosemide*, so that's completely normal for me."

No wonder she looked at me strangely when I asked her if there was any blood in her faeces. Shit, I think I very nearly just left a stroke patient at home! I don't think its gastroenteritis at all, I think it's a posterior stroke. Central vertigo*, sickness and a posterior headache, are all a textbook trio for this rare kind of event.

I perform a number of neurological assessments on route to the CT scanner on blue lights, and it's here I also notice she has bilateral nystagmus*; another classic sign of a posterior stroke. Within ten minutes we arrive at the CT scanner in our local hospital, and we suddenly begin to notice her pulse pressure* increasing, which is the first sign of Cushing's triad*. This also suggests a haemorrhagic stroke, as opposed to a clot. As I wait silently in the corner of the room in anticipation to see the CT scan, a black and white moving picture of the patient's brain pings up in front of me. On it is a black cloud measuring approximately one centremeter, which is located at the posterior aspect of her cranium. This is blood from a burst aneurysm, pooling into the brain matter. Unfortunately, as the patient awoke with these symptoms she has no onset time, which means she will not undergo any brain surgery. However, as the haematoma is still small, she can be treated with supportive measures. This means she will be administered anticonvulsants*, beta blockers* or angiotensin converting enzyme (ACE) inhibitors*, and osmotic diuretics*. These will manage the symptoms, whilst helping lower the patient's blood pressure to prevent the cranial bloody mess from growing any larger. She will then remain as an inpatient until eventually the blood is redistributed back around her body. At least that's the plan.

Thankfully, seeing as the patient awoke with her symptoms, the treatment wouldn't have changed if we had have immediately identified the aneurysm on scene, and got her to hospital. But it certainly gives me a stark reminder to always have posterior stokes in the back of my mind.

CHAPTER THIRTY TWO:

Utility Room

We're in the biggest, grandest house I think I've ever been called to! We walk through three hallways before we are lead by the patient to her living room/ballroom. The grand, ornate fireplace almost takes up the entirety of one of her humongous walls. It's hand crafted, intricate architecture spreading itself across the room making itself known, like an unmanaged overgrown fungus in an unmanaged woods, but prettier. I'm certain the rug is the same size as my entire house, and the grand piano, paintings and sculptures must be worth millions. It's like we've been called to Sir Elton John's stately home. After taking it all in for a moment, gawping in absolute awe and envy, one of us finally gets back to the patient's complaint.

It isn't me.

"So what's the problem today?" My crew mate asks. I'm working with my old mentor today, it's so nice to have some familiarity.

"I just don't feel like I'm coping, don't get me wrong I'm not depressed, I'd never even dream of harming myself, I am just so lonely lately." She answers.

"I understand" my previous mentor sympathises. "Do you belong to any clubs or anything, or have any friends locally?"

I'm half listening, but half still mesmerised by the patient's home.

"The only friend I have lives in the utility room, and she doesn't come to visit me very often."

"Pardon?" She has my full attention now.

"In the utility room?" I question.

"Yes, she's my lodger"

My crew mate and I look at one another bewildered, yet curious. She can't actually have a friend living in the utility room, can she? Maybe she really isn't coping and has lost touch with reality.

"Umm, I'm sorry madam, I'm not entirely sure it's feasible to live in a utility room. Is it?"

"Yes it is, don't be ridiculous, she's my lodger, go and look if you don't believe me!" She retorts loudly.

We're just too curious not to look. Besides, what if there is someone in there? Maybe she's keeping somebody hostage and calls her a lodger? I try not get too carried away with myself. As we get our torches out and walk cautiously into the disused room, where a layer of dust covers the old kitchen appliances, I can't help but be reminded of Mrs Haversham's house in Dicken's *Great Expectations*.

"You go first" I say to my crew mate.

"No you go first, you're older"

"We'll go together"

"Ok"

As we make our way to the end of the dark uninviting room, it is apparent nobody is residing here, so I shout a quick 'hello' with no response, to prove this to our patient, then start heading back to the living room. Whilst we walk back and consider how we're going to manage this situation now, we all of a sudden hear a 'hello' coming from behind us.

"What the fuck!" Cries my crew mate in sheer terror, whilst I scream and we both leap backwards. There, standing before our eyes is a middle aged woman in her pyjamas, wondering what all the commotion is about. Behind her is an open door leading into a beautiful annex. A door we failed to notice, as there is a lifetime worth of coats hanging on it.

"Can I help you?" The woman asks.

We stand there in silence, jaws dropped, absolutely gobsmacked. Usually I'm very good at containing myself, but this time neither of us can help but laugh out loud. Luckily, we are joined by our original patient.

"You thought I was making it up didn't you?" She laughs.

"Umm… not making it up, just that you were more poorly than we originally thought."

Half hour later, after the four of us have had a cup of tea and a good chat about the patient's not quite so severe mental health, we email the GP and advise the patient and her lodger to join clubs, to conquer their loneliness. When we get back into the cab of the ambulance, we let out a huge belt of laughter that we'd been holding in for all that time.

CHAPTER THIRTY THREE:
PV bleed

Another NQP and I have been sent to a per vaginal (PV) bleed in town and that's all the information we've been given. The job comes in as a category three, so we don't rush; and besides, the last PV bleed I went to was a young woman having her first menstrutive cycle. As we arrive on scene and are led into the conservatory by the patients husband, we are both surprised and disappointed to see she's lost a lot of blood, seeing as she's twelve weeks pregnant. The couple seem unusually calm though, as we estimate the patient's blood loss and quickly perform a full set of vital signs.

"This has happened before," admits the patient.

"Twice" continues the husband, "last time she lost our baby she was admitted to the intensive care unit (ICU) and needed a blood transfusion, this was our last attempt at IVF".
Our hearts sink for them both.

"Well, we'll try get you to hospital and stop the bleeding long before it gets to that point this time, ok." I try to reassure them.

Our patient becomes more and more distressed though as she soon realises she can't stand. Where she's been bleeding continuously and has been sat down for a long period, the clotted blood has dried and quite literally glued her to her seat. Before we tackle this problem though, we decide to cannulate. Despite her blood pressure being stable at the moment, she has already told us she required blood transfusions last time, so we're not going to take that risk. Neither of us have any luck whatsoever though, 'I don't believe it! I haven't missed a cannula in months and now I'm on my third attempt. What's wrong with me?' I think to myself. My crew mate is in the same boat on the opposite arm, so before long we decide we can't keep stabbing this poor lady with needles when she's stable, let's just get her in the ambulance. We pile multiple incontinence pads onto our carry chair in preparation, then gradually un-stick her from her seat.

To start with, she's unsurprisingly very reluctant to stand, but once she's been set free from the dried mess, she quickly throws herself onto our carry chair. In doing so though, piles and piles of clots and fresh blood splash onto her lino flooring, leaving her husband as white as a sheet. I think he thinks their foetus is somewhere amongst those clots, and he wouldn't necessarily be wrong. I am convinced we dispose of these clots, either by flushing them down the toilet or putting them in the clinical waste bin at hospital. This was what I was told and had witnessed as a student, but my colleague and friend is sure we take the clots with us and hand them over to the nurse in charge with the patient, in a more emotional response. I reluctantly agree to bring them, I'd prefer take them and not need them, than flush them away and later find out they were required. What's the worst that could happen with us taking them with us? We'll just dispose of them there if they're not needed.

I continue measuring her vital signs on route, particularly her blood pressure, and provide a pre-alert to the receiving hospital, as its evident how quickly she deteriorated last time and could again.

When we're half way to ED and I'm in the back of the ambulance alone with the patient and her husband, her blood pressure drops substantially, reading 90/55*. It was 140 systolic only a few minutes prior, 'maybe it's playing up again, I'll redo it' I tell myself. 80/40.
"Pull over!" I shout through the cubby hole glass window separating the cab from the back of the ambulance.

"We really need to get a line in now" I tell my colleague, as she enters through the side door. Our patient is a harrowing shade of grey. We lie her flat and spring her legs up in the air in an attempt to raise her blood pressure, but what she really needs is a saline drip into one of her veins and Transexamic acid (TXA); neither of which we can administer until we successfully cannulate. Well actually what she really needs is another blood transfusion, but we don't carry blood products on the road.

We both attack each arm again and again in a desperate attempt to get some access. I find the more I fail, the worse my confidence gets and the worse I cannulate, so I try hard to treat every cannulation like my first time, and swallow my pride. Finally, out of the blue I get flashback. I'm in! We quickly get her started on a saline drip and look to one another anxiously whilst drawing up the TXA. Neither of us have administered this drug before, so we frantically check our drug calculations and indications. Once we're as confident as we can be of our dosages, we plunge the syringe slowly into the cannula, one minute at a time, praying it raises her blood pressure.

As my colleague hops back into the cab and quickly drives us to resus, I ring the hospital to update them on the patient's deterioration. Her husband is clutching her clammy hand trying to stay strong and hold back the tears now, whilst the patient lies still with her eyes closed.

Thankfully, on arrival at resus the TXA and fluids seem to have taken effect. Her blood pressure is now 110 systolic, she has her colour back in her cheeks and she's asking to be sat back upright. "Is THIS the one you rang in?" The nurse asks.

"The TXA and saline seem to have taken effect better than we had expected" I reply.

The agency nurse sighs and helps us transfer the patient onto a hospital bed. There are so many fantastic, pleasant members of staff here, how come I never get to hand over to any of them? She isn't very impressed we brought the patients bloody clots with us either.

CHAPTER THIRTY FOUR:
I Really Am A 'Shit' Magnet

Literally just as my bum cheeks touch the rim of the toilet seat and I start expelling, my radio goes off, and it's a category one, cardiac arrest. Of course it is! I try my best to hurry but the toilet just isn't flushing. I try again but it's apparent it's blocked, and it's filling up quickly. In a panic I close the toilet seat and leave the cubicle in a calm manner as if I am just as clueless to the entire situation as the next person. The next person though, waiting outside the door just so happens to be my manager. I don't give him any eye contact as I mumble a hello and rush to the ambulance. The only poor excuse I have is it's a category one call. The screen reads 'confirmed cardiac arrest, fifty one year old male in the centre of town'. I hate public jobs, the world and his wife are almost always there, and always desperate to tell me they've just completed their first aid at work training and know all everything about what we do. Or they stand there and film the whole event in the hope they'll sell it to the papers for millions! When we arrive, my expectations are met perfectly. A bystander comes running up to the ambulance before its even stopped, shouting:

"He's dead! He's dead!" then disappears back into the crowd.

We can't even see the patient amongst the many frantic bodies, so we request police, grab all the kit we think we might need, and make our way through the crowd. I am so gob smacked at what I find when we reach the patient, I actually stop for a second in disbelief and try take in what I'm witnessing. The bystander who ran into the moving ambulance shouting 'he's dead' is now bouncing up and down on the patient's chest performing CPR on our regular caller, who is very much alive and conscious. Between blows the patient cries "fuck off" trying to throw punches, but the newly trained first aider is having none of it.

"It's ok, calm down, I'm saving your life" he shouts.

The patient who has no fixed address (NFA) often rings for himself from the local phone box, but I've never once seen him in this situation before! I can almost understand why bystanders are feeling the need to watch this. Still only almost!

My crew mate who used to be in the military, quickly prises the gentleman from our patient and tells all the filming bystanders to politely piss off. I cancel our request for police assistance pretty quickly, as my ECA seems to have managed the situation very well singlehandedly.

Now most of the bystanders have subsided - including the newly qualified first aider attempting CPR on our live patient - we try to establish from the intoxicated gentleman what's actually gone on, but all we're met by is slurred:

"Fuck off's" and "you c**** can't help me" as he staggers to his feet.

Every time he attempts to stand though he stumbles to the ground in an intoxicated mess, landing on his paralytic cranium. It's obvious now that he's also been prolifically incontinent. His three pairs of trousers are covered in cold, odorous urine sticking to his calves, whilst wet diarrhoea seeps down the inside of his trousers into his socks and shoes. I assume he's wearing three pairs due to the cold and living on the streets.

What's more, where he's been bounced on numerous times, the faeces has spread up his back and dried into his long, knotted hair. What really makes me cringe though is the trail of human faeces across the grass where the public take their children and walk their dogs. I honestly don't know where to start, but I know he definitely needs to attend hospital, for so many reasons. Thankfully for us, he lacks capacity, and his GCS quickly drops due to the amount of alcohol he has consumed, so we are able to lift him onto the stretcher calmly and take him to a very unimpressed ED.

The second we finish cleaning the ambulance and press clear outside the hospital, we are sent to our next job, and it's a ninety one year old with diarrhoea and vomiting. This is now the third dealing I've had with shit today! When we arrive, the patient hasn't vomited at all, nor does she feel nauseous. She just feels like she's probably taken one too many laxatives, and I agree looking at the scene before me, holding my breath.

The ninety one year old is extremely distressed, and for good reason. She's slipped on her rug causing no injuries, but has been on the cold floor for so long, she's opened her bowels profusely ,after self administering laxatives for the past three days. We mask up and put our aprons on for the second time today and like our last job, wonder where to begin.

"Oh my, please help me," she sobs, tears rolling down her cheeks. "I'm sorry, I can't get up, I'm so sorry"

"Please don't apologise," I reassure her "absolutely nothing to apologise for I promise. Of course we're going to help you."

As lovely as she is though and as much as my heart really does sink for her, it really does smell putrid. What on earth has she been eating? Keeping an expressionless face and wearing a mask over my gagging mouth to save her dignity really pay me dividends here, as I don't want to risk offending our patient. It must be so mortifying for her, I can't even imagine. There is no way I want her to witness my over stimulated senses. She does however notice my uncovered teary eyes, but I think she thinks that's because of the sadness of the situation, rather than the smell actually physically making me cry!

Eventually, two sets of PPE, a bath towel, an entire pack of clinical wipes and some bleach later, the patient smells strongly of cotton sheets; at least that's what the bottle of air fragrance reckons she smells of. The frail ninety one year old is tucked up in her dressing gown next to a burning fire with a hot cup of cocoa, awaiting her evening carer. What a difference. It feels so fantastic to see her content after the ordeal. She's so unbelievably thankful and apologetic, my heart melts for her. Sometimes it's not about bringing people back from the dead, it's about wiping a ninety one year olds defecated cheeks.

CHAPTER THIRTY FIVE:

Anaphylaxis

Just as I take a bite into the donut I've literally just treated myself to, a job comes in, and it's my turn to drive so I can't even eat it on route. It says on the screen 'anaphylaxis'. Now true anaphylaxis is life threatening as it often results in two or more of the bodily systems becoming shocked, eventually causing multi-organ failure, but most of the public are unaware of this. Most people assume it solely effects the respiratory system or the skin on the face, however it actually can also cause hypovolaemic* and cardiovascular shock, as well as gastrointestinal and dermatological symptoms.

I've never been to a real anaphylactic patient before. I've been to plenty of patients who thought they were in anaphylactic shock with their hives rash, or itchy tongue, but none of them have been true anaphylaxis. I try to not be cynical as I rush to scene. One day I know I really will be sent to a real time critical patient whose epi-pen isn't working, and there's every chance this could be it. I go over drug algorithms and calculations in my head whilst speeding past the parked cars on blue lights. I think I remember everything.

When the husband answers the door I can already hear the patient's noisy breathing coming from the bathroom. She has a stridor*. As I rush upstairs to find my first real anaphylactic patient it's exactly as

I imagined it would be. Her entire face is flushed and swollen; her lips, tongue and eyes the worst. Her inflamed purple lips take up almost a third of her entire face and are hot to touch, whilst her swollen dark eyes stream; partly because of the histamine response* and partly due to fear. She's leant forward over the bath in a tripod position*, desperately trying to inspire air into her closing airways. Moreover, I cannot feel a radial pulse, which means her blood pressure is so dangerously low her peripherals aren't being adequately perfused. I know I have to work really quickly here before she becomes so deprived of oxygen and hypotensive* she loses consciousness. I always thought I'd be silently terrified in this situation, I've just got very good at hiding my fears, however I actually feel ok. I know exactly what to do and when to do it, so I quickly crack on and utilise my training.

Whilst my ECA starts drawing up a strong nebuliser to dilate the lungs air canals, I draw up a cocktail of other drugs to help reverse the anaphylactic process. Adrenaline first, straight into her deltoid muscle*, which is a powerful drug stimulating the widening of the airways and the narrowing of the blood vessels, to improve blood pressure; amongst many other affects. In the fight or flight response, this drug stimulates the fight, and will therefore aid in stabilising the patient's abnormal vital signs. Next, I administer an antihistamine and a steroid to prevent the further release of histamine, preventing the condition from worsening.

By now her bathroom is an absolute tip! Used epipens, airway packaging, sharps boxes -hers and ours-, our emergency kit, gauze from the intramuscular (IM) injections and a defibrillator - just in case - all scattered within the confined space. I don't have any time to worry about that yet though, her condition isn't improving despite the three strong, lifesaving medications flushing through her circulation. She's still deprived of oxygen, has no radial pulse, and is becoming more and more cyanotic*, centrally as well as peripherally now. She looks like she's just sprinted two marathons, but bluer! I can't administer her more antihistamines or steroids, she's already had the maximum required dose, but I can administer more IM adrenaline, which has no maximum dose providing it is given five minutes apart. When another five minutes passes though and there's still little improvement, I make the conscious decision to get her on the ambulance and get moving.

Her allergen is balloons, which she came into contact with at a neighbour's birthday party. She certainly isn't being exposed to balloons any longer, so I'm unsure why the drugs I'm administering aren't yet taking effect. I don't have time to sit and think about it though, so I scoop up all our kit and the mess we made, and get the patient to resus as quickly as possible.

Thankfully, ten minutes before arriving at hospital following two more IM adrenalines, she improves. Her breathing becomes slower and less noisy, her blood pressure increases and her lips reduce in size substantially. By the time we arrive at hospital she's even talking to us in full sentences, but is as high as a kite on adrenaline. She may feel great but she's going to need to be monitored very closely in resus for a while yet. To have this many adrenaline administrations is like having twenty energy drinks in one afternoon. I don't think I appreciated how many adrenalines I actually administered her until the nurse replies 'three mg?!' before I finished my handover, but on this rare occasion, she really did need all of those. If she hadn't have received them, her airways could have closed completely.

It feels so damned good to see her breathing effectively with a good, strong blood pressure when I get ready to leave, but I do feel slightly guilty for the resus staff, leaving her here in this manic, adrenaline fuelled state, which she will likely stay in for the rest of the day.

CHAPTER THIRTY SIX:

Crazy Shit You Only See On Night Shifts

You really do see the craziest shit on night shifts, stuff you'd never see in the daytime when the majority of the public are working in their nine to five jobs. As we make our way to hopefully our final job of the night, we suddenly notice a lady who's most likely in her late forties sweeping the roundabout with her broomstick, in her pyjamas. Its three in the morning and the peak of the summer, so we have no idea what she's sweeping, there's certainly not any fallen leaves around. If we weren't on our way to a category one call we would stop, so instead we inform Control in case they feel it necessary to contact the police. It's not only comical and unusual sights we see on night shifts though, we are currently travelling to a twenty one year old suicide attempt. This is an all too common occurrence, and almost always at night. As we tear down the empty streets on blue lights we receive a further update. It's a confirmed hanging.

As we pull up there are already two other ambulances and an RRV on scene, their blue lights lighting up the entire street and surrounding areas, like the aftermath of a murder scene in a horror film. Neighbours look out of their windows, then quickly hide behind their curtains when they realise we can see them. Others aren't so diplomatic and come running out their front door with hair rollers in, asking: 'What's happened?' We've woken up the entire street, but we can't and won't tell any one of them what we've been sent to. Seeing as there are already three crews here, we don't carry in any kit, they will have all they need inside, and probably more. So we hurry to the front door empty handed. When I say hurried, we are trained to not run. Instead, we take that extra few seconds to compose ourselves and make it safely to the scene. We're of no use whatsoever to the patient if we trip and injure ourselves, make silly mistakes, or are too breathless to perform adequate CPR.

As we enter the property we initially struggle to fit through the front door as there is a full resus underway in the hallway, so we attempt to clamber over kit and furniture before listening to the clinical handover. The twenty one year old was found by his ten year old brother hanging by a piece of electrical cable from the stair banister. The ten year old had attempted to cut the wire in an effort to get his deceased brother down onto even ground, when their mother heard the commotion and came out to discover the horrifying scene. The first crew to arrive just ten minutes ahead of us, took the cable from around the patient's neck where his brother cut him down and commenced a resuscitation attempt. He has been in asystole throughout. One crew member is talking with the patients family, whilst two are about to intubate, two alternate chest compressions, and one is administering drugs. I offer to assist with chest compressions to prevent compression fatigue - which is easier said than done - whilst my crew mate goes to speak with the family along with the other clinician. There is barely enough room for the crews here already though, who are squatting in some pretty peculiar positions just trying to fit around the patient, so we come up with a plan. In one swift movement I will alternate with one of the ECAs -who has lost all feeling in his legs - between chest compressions, whilst our colleague continues intubating. We time it perfectly, thankfully.

We give him everything we've got, adrenaline, high flow oxygen forced directly into his still lungs, and powerful CPR, but we receive nothing back other than a flat line. When we get to twenty minutes of asystole we would normally stop and pronounce the patient as deceased, but one crew member is not willing to stop.

"He's twenty one for God's sake!" He retorts loudly.

None of us are going to argue, but we all know that we're not getting this patient back; including the member of staff wanting to call it I think. He's gone, and further efforts are futile. Nobody ever comes back after twenty minutes of asystole. Eventually, when the body appears to be getting colder and stiffer, and there is too much resistance in to bag*, we call it. Death confirmed. The patient's mother shrieks with grief as she hears those dreaded words. It's a heart wrenching, blood churning cry that fills the entire house, and can't be mistaken for anything else. We all clear up and rid the body of equipment in utter silence, a lump in all our throats. It's not an absolute necessity we all remain on scene now, but seeing as Control say they have no jobs stacking up, we all decide to stay to provide support to one another and debrief as a team.

Collectively we extricate the twenty one year old onto the stretcher and into the ambulance for his family to come in one by one to say their goodbyes. His Mum comes in first sobbing, legs like jelly. "You selfish boy!" She sobs uncontrollably. "You've ruined our lives, we love you so much" We leave the ambulance to give them some privacy and enter another ambulance for a debrief.

I'm always asked 'What's the worst thing you've ever seen?' by excited members of the public when I dubiously tell them I'm a paramedic. It's like they expect me to say I saw someone get blown up and they lost all four limbs but miraculously survived to tell the tale, or I saw brain matter all over the dual carriageway after a decapitation following a fifteen car pile up. It's none of those ridiculous things, it's watching a grieving Mother say goodbye to the body of her beloved twenty one year old son. Hearing those cries is sickening to the stomach. And knowing his ten year old brother will have to live with the image of his dead older brother, his role model, hanging over the banister he uses every day, for the rest of his life. I can see gore and trauma at museums and online if I really choose to. It's not that which breaks my heart for a brief moment in time.

After we feel we've done everything we possibly can for the broken family, one crew remains on scene to await the police - purely because it's an unexpected death - and the rest of us try going to get a McDonalds breakfast to debrief properly over some food. Unsurprisingly though, every single one of us gets called to another job before we even make it to the end of the street.

CHAPTER THIRTY SEVEN:
Hunger Strike

I'm in the most peculiar situation I've been in to date I think, so much so I'm having to ring my manager for support, as I'm completely clueless on what to do next. We've been called to a residential home for adults with severe learning disabilities, and our patient today is refusing to eat or drink. She has been on these hunger strikes before and last time was admitted to ICU for severe electrolyte imbalances. Today marks the second day our patient has not eaten or drunk anything whatsoever in another strike. Despite not presenting with any abnormal signs or symptoms, as of yet, care staff are concerned she will quickly head in the same direction as last time, only three months previously. So they dialled 999.

On entering the patient's bedroom she has her whole body and her head wrapped up in her duvet with only her hands on show.

"Hi, I'm Georgia and this is…" We don't get a chance to introduce ourselves before the moving duvet shouts for us to "piss off!"

"It's ok, we're here to help. What a beautiful bedroom, did you paint these pictures on the wall yourself?"

Just as I finish my sentence a woman in her late forties emerges from under the sheets, red faced and raging. Then a hairbrush comes flying towards my head with another "piss off". I don't bat an eyelid, I've seen this a hundred times before with my sister and in my previous line of work with autistic children. Besides, I've had far worse thrown at me than a hairbrush. TV remotes, vases, laptops. Not only directed at me by the way. Anyone who gets in the way of a meltdown is likely to get something thrown at their heads.

"No need to do that," I say calmly, trying to show her I trust her and I'm not scared of her. I sit down next to her and start talking to my crew mate from across the room:

"These are beautiful paintings, I really wish I could paint like that, don't you?"

"I'd love to paint like that, they're incredible, especially that one of the dog" my colleague replies.

We continue this conversation for around twenty minutes before we start including the patient, in the hope she's been listening and calmed down a little by now.

"Has that dog on your wall got a name?" I ask.

"Bog off" she responds aggressively. Clearly distraction isn't working, so I try a new tactic.

"Do you know why we're here today?"

"No" she responds.

"We're here because your carers are concerned about you, they say you're not eating or drinking."

"They don't care about me, they smell, and so do you!" She shouts. I haven't even come into contact with faeces today which is unusual for me at the end of a twelve hour shift; when people say they're shit magnets, they often mean to trauma and gore.

In fairness to our patient, every single one of us is wearing a different perfume today and I was always told when working in a special needs school never to wear perfume, as the kids often perceive the smell differently to how we do, often stronger and/or more offensively.

"I understand, it must be frustrating having two strangers come into your bedroom smelling funny and telling you what to do, I wouldn't like that very much either, but I promise you, we just want to help you." I tell our patient, attempting to understand her way of thinking and to reassure her. "How about you tell me what your favourite drink is? If you could choose anything what would it be? Then we'll get off your back."

"BOOOOG OFF!" She shouts back at me at the top of her lungs, whilst a full bottle of water now comes flying towards both of our heads. "You're not on my back and you never will be!" Special needs patients often take things very, very literally, so if you say you'll get off their back, you must already be on their back, or if you say you're burying your head in the sand or you're splitting your sides laughing, they'll look at you in a very strange manner.

We decide to give her a break and speak with the care staff in the office, they know her better than anyone else does and know what works for her, they live with her. However, when we tell them this, they inform us that everything that usually works for the patient hasn't for the last forty eight hours. Normally one member of staff - who differs each time - is able to calm her and get her eating and drinking again in no time, but this time nobody is getting through to her.

"This is usual behaviour for her" they inform us "but she usually responds well to at least one of us. This time not only is she not responding to us, she's also a lot more irritable than she normally would be".

This makes me wonder if she's got a brewing infection or electrolyte imbalance already, making her confused and agitated, but she won't let any of us anywhere near her to perform a single vital sign, so there's no way of telling.

Whilst waiting for management to arrive, I decide to ring the GP for advice and a potential hospital admission. Unfortunately, I cannot assess her capacity at present so I have to assume she lacks capacity, as I would with any patient who cannot, or will not, answer a series of basic questions, including explaining the likely outcome of their decision not to attend ED, autistic, 'neurotypical' or otherwise. If she lacks capacity there is a small chance we can get her admitted onto a ward in her best interest, so this is how I go about my conversation with the GP. The GP though -although admitting we're in a very difficult situation- voices my initial unsaid suspicions, that we cannot admit a patient when there may be absolutely nothing medically wrong with them. And seeing as she won't let us perform any observations, we can't take her in 'just in case'. Although I'm disappointed with his response as I thought that might be our only way out of this difficult situation, I agree with him entirely. Just as I get off the phone though, my manager arrives. Thank goodness!

We explain the situation to the lead paramedic (my manager) and pray he has a solution. As we all walk into the bedroom he starts from scratch.

"So why are you not eating?" He asks calmly.

"It tastes yucky!"

I decide to leave them to it, there really is no point all three of us being in there overwhelming her, so I sit in the doorway unseen and start typing up the paperwork. Whilst doing so the carers come rushing in with the telephone.

"It's your boyfriend!" One carer shouts out enthusiastically, handing the phone to our patient.

Another care home comes to visit once a week and our patient seems to have taken a shine to one of the residents. All of a sudden, her entire demeanour and voice changes from loud and defensive to chirpy, carefree and enthusiastic, and she talks to him like they could talk to one another for hours. This could be our way in. When the carers take the phone back ten minutes later, I try again.

"Your boyfriend wants you to be healthy and strong doesn't he?"

I am just met by a cushion to the groin, so I go back into the office to complete the rest of the paperwork and consider my life choices! I'm starting the think the patient really doesn't like me very much.

I'm astounded when five minutes later I walk into the patient's bedroom to find her and the lead paramedic sat chatting and laughing together over a cup of tea and biscuits. It's like a completely different patient. Within a few minutes we're all sat in a circle like at a little tea party, drinking our hot drinks, helping the patient fill out her menu choices for this evening. Moreover, she's let the lead paramedic perform a full set of vital signs, and to our pleasant surprise, everything comes back stable.

"How did you do that?" I asked the lead paramedic, and saviour(!) when we leave the scene.

"I really thought I tried everything."

"I think it was just a change of face. The only difference between me and everyone that tried previously, is that they were all woman, and I'm a man. Maybe she needed a male authoritative voice to reason with her this time… and of course, my fantastic personality!" He laughs.

I agree with him and am obviously pleased at the outcome, but go home slightly miffed that I couldn't do it myself. Ah well, another life saved!

CHAPTER THIRTY EIGHT:

Do You Really Get Sent To That?

We're often called to the military base so we usually locate it no problem, seeing as we've been here hundreds of times. However, today the satnav has taken us to a different entrance, and we're well and truly lost. This entrance, that neither of us have come across before, is locked up like Fort Knox and there are no guards at the gate like there are at the other entrance. What's more, it's the middle of the night, so where our co-ordinates are plotting just the other side of the barbed wire twelve foot fence, we can't see a thing past an overgrown field with our mediocre torches, so we contact Control.

"That is strange," Control replies after I explain the situation. "A young man has rung from a phone box on the military camp to say it's stinging when he urinates."

Not a medical emergency then. Neither of us even realised the military bases even have phone boxes.

After driving around in circles it quickly becomes apparent that the only way in is via the main entrance we know all too well. From there we can drive to the co-ordinates directly through the camp, and we should be on the right side of the fence, and the field, so that's exactly where we head. After the ambulance is checked for weapons and bombs by muscley soldiers with machine guns on the gate, we drive to the co-ordinates on the lookout for phone boxes. I'm not entirely sure whether I should be scared or attracted to the soldiers.

Following the satnav to our intended destination though is not quite as easy as we expect. It keeps telling us to turn right onto overgrown meadows and straight on, which is directly into a block of terraced houses, so we estimate the route by how well we know the camp already. In other words we make the whole thing up as we go, and are thankful it's just a urinary tract infection (UTI) we're being sent to. Before long our route mapping appears to be lacking, as we end up back at the main gate, met with blank expressions on the soldiers faces. You couldn't make this up. Finally, after driving around in circles for twenty minutes we reach the piece of land where the co-ordinates are plotting. We're highly disappointed to be in the field just the other side of the abandoned entrance we were at earlier this evening though. We really weren't missing anything with our mediocre torches, it really is just an abandoned field without a single telephone box in sight. Instead just a three foot electric cylinder with a barbed wire fence around it reading 'Keep Off!'

Just as we get hold of Control to find out if this is some sort of prank, a loud knock comes out of nowhere on the passenger side door of the ambulance. It scares the absolute living shit out of the pair of us, we almost jump out of our skins. I quickly shine a torch out of my window and am met with the confused face of a soldier. I'm face to face with the roaming patrol, and we've just been driving around on his land in an ambulance in circles for the last half hour, before stopping in a deserted field.

"Can I help you?" he asks, looking unimpressed by how startled we are to see him.

"We've been called to a young man with a urinary tract infection (UTI) who called from a phone box on camp. The co-ordinates for the phone box are plotting right here," I tell him.

"We don't have phone boxes here…. Wait, what's a UTI?" he responds.

"A urinary tract infection, also known as a water infection."

"People actually call you for that shit?" The soldier laughs, seeing the funny side now.

"Apparently so!" We reply back.

"Well you're more than welcome to keep looking for him, but do us a favour, if you find the pussy, send him my way!"

CHAPTER THIRTY NINE:
Everyone Has The Right To Make A Bad Decision

We've been sent to one of our regulars for our first job this evening. I've never actually been to her before, but I've seen her in ED previously, and my crew mate has been called out to her on numerous occasions. Apparently, despite a social worker and psychiatric nurse visiting the patient every day, the forty year old still rings 999 most evenings for suicidal thoughts. She's never yet actioned these thoughts, but often tells attending crews that she will as soon as they leave her property. What's more, she refuses hospital each and every time, which is fundamentally the only place of safety for her in the middle of the night, when she often calls. This puts crews in a very difficult situation. We can't drag her out of her home and into the ambulance, that would be kidnapping as she has full mental capacity. But at the same time, she tells us she'll make an attempt on her life as soon as we leave. Technically, provided we're 100% certain she has full mental capacity, which she often does, we can leave scene and get her to sign a refusal form. Everybody has the right to make what we think is a bad decision, who are we to say their decision is the wrong one, that's just mine, and most of society's opinion. That though doesn't take into account how we'll sleep at night if she does attempt and succeed in committing suicide. Not to mention we'll be asked to attend Coroners Court where we'd be scrutinised and have to justify every word, action and decision we made. For these reasons and these reasons only, no crew wants to draw the short straw and be called to this patient, and tonight it's my first time. After a few colourful phrases from my crew mate when we see her name pop up on our screen, we make our way to her flat.

As we ring her doorbell we hear a faint voice saying "Come in" and are met by the one and only.

"How can we help?"

"I want to kill myself" she whimpers.

After asking all the usual questions: 'How long have you been feeling this way?' 'Do you have a good support network?' 'Do you have a plan and the means to make an attempt on your life?' And so on and so forth, we are totally honest with our patient.

"I can see you're really struggling and clearly in a lot of emotional pain, and we're here to help you, but we're not trained in mental health," I confess. "The hospital however, have trained professionals on call that really can help you, so the best course of action would be to let us take you up there."

"No!" the patient resists, "I don't like hospitals."

"Neither do I particularly, but it's our only option this time of the night, other than leaving you here alone."

"If you leave me along I'll swallow all my pills and it will be all your fault," she threatens. (There it is).

"Then let us run you up the hospital then, eh? They can help you."

"No!"

We go round in circles for what feels like hours with no solution. We've both tried every approach in the book, from distraction to persuasion, to being brutally honest about the situation, but it's still very apparent she's not going to come to hospital with us, and we can't drag her there kicking and screaming! So we ring the crisis team. The phone rings and rings with no response for over thirty minutes! So in the meantime I dig out the direct number for her community mental health team (CMHT) in the blind hope it'll direct me to an emergency out of hours line.

When they don't answer either, we make a plan on what we are going to do if neither contacts get back to us. We really would have exhausted all options by this point, so we come to the conclusion we can only contact our manager to ensure there really is no alternative and get her to sign a refusal before we head on to our next patient, hoping to God she doesn't actually commit suicide. Just then though, after spending almost two hours with the patient, we get a call back from the CMHT, where I left a message. We've struck gold! Her designated psychiatric nurse just so happens to be the emergency clinician on call this evening, and he wishes to speak with his patient, so we promptly hand her the telephone. We wait in hope and anticipation whilst the two of them remain deep in conversation for a further thirty minutes.

"Ok, I'll come to hospital." She eventually agrees, handing the phone back to us.

I almost shout with joy, but I refrain.

The hospital staff aren't particularly thrilled to see we've brought them their frequent caller, but they understand it was the only safe option available to us. Besides, we were instructed to do so by her CMHT. Unfortunately though, the hospital are now left in just as a difficult situation as we were. The patient leaves her cubicle every five minutes whilst waiting for the psychiatric team, hounding the nurses and patients alike, asking when she'll be discharged. The poor sick patients with broken bones and chest pains are left confused and angry when the psychiatric patient becomes aggressive towards them when they can't tell her when she'll be allowed home. Moreover she has a tendency to wander off endlessly before returning to her cubicle, with no idea where she's been. Sometimes I wonder what it actually takes to be admitted to a psychiatric hospital, surely this fits the bill perfectly?

On our return to ED with our next patient of the night, an hour or so after we dropped off our psychiatric patient, we see her sat at the side of the ambulance bay, slumped over as if unresponsive. On approaching her though it is immediately clear she is not unresponsive at all, she comes at us with her fists through the windows, shouting about how us morons aren't helping her. We can't hang around, we have to think about the safety of our current patient now, so we continue into the ED. The nurses quickly inform us she is sat out there by choice, despite numerous attempts of trying to bring her back into her cubicle where has not yet been discharged. She remains in this position for the majority of our night shift, it's a good job it's not a cold night out! Finally, on driving to the hospital at 07:00 ready to admit our final patient of the night, she has disappeared. We can only imagine she got transported home by the police, or got bored and went home herself, ready to do the whole thing again this evening.

***

I don't believe my eyes. Our regular psych patient who we admitted only five days ago is being rushed into resus following a hefty diazepam overdose. In ten plus years of dialling 999, informing us she's going to end her life, but never actually doing so, she's in resus being ventilated. We're all gob smacked, nobody believed that after ten years of threatening she'd actually take the leap and do it, but here she is. As much as I feel the upmost sympathy for her, I can't help but think how lucky we were to speak to her psychiatric nurse who convinced her to attend hospital. Without which, we would likely be in Coroners Court for the next six months, I'm sure questioning even our own rational decisions at times.

CHAPTER FOURTY:
Gullible

Its midnight and I'm in the middle of an RRV night shift. In some ways it's great! I'm my own boss so I can choose when I write my paperwork, what I write and what shop I go to to buy myself some dinner and an obligatory midnight snack, but in many ways it's so much more stressful. I can't confirm drug dosages with anyone except myself or ask for a bit of healthy advice from my crew mate. I can't even have the ridiculous immature banter I often have with my ECA that gets us both through the night. It's just damned right boring and lonely, to say the least.

The radio has just gone off and I've been called to a young male who's been found at the side of the road who has dislocated his left hip, left ankle and right shoulder. It's rare to dislocate so many joints with no other apparent trauma, so I can only assume he has something like brittle bones disease, but that won't make the pain any less excruciating.

On scanning the road where the co-ordinates are plotting, I fail to spot anyone, despite driving up and down the well lit street on numerous occasions, so I get out my torch and start looking for him on foot. It's freezing. The cars already have ice on their windscreens and I'm shivering, even in my thick layers and Hi-Viz jacket, so I can't begin to imagine how cold the poor patient is.

Just as I get back to the car to inform Control there is no sign of him and turn my headlights on, I spot a dark figure lying on the grass. How did I not notice him before? He's right there on the grass verge I drove past on multiple occasions with my full beam lighting up the entire street. As I approach and introduce myself, I'm surprised to see he isn't cold at all, and not appearing to be in a great deal of pain.

"Hi I'm Georgia, I'm so sorry about the wait in the cold."

"Ah no worries, I'm not cold, nor in much pain" he chuckles. "I've just dislocated my hip, ankle and shoulder again walking home from a mates house."

Even so, I quickly request back up to get him out the cold and onto an ambulance where we can assess him properly. It's extremely busy tonight, so the only other paramedic that's not currently with another patient in the entire county apparently. is the specialist paramedic on the car at my local station. I bet someone jinxed it earlier by using the phrase 'it's quiet'. When I explain to Control that I really need an ambulance to start assessing this patient though, they cleverly take the specialist paramedic off the car and put him on the single truck, single manned, so that when he arrives, we'll be a double crewed ambulance; with a spare car, but we can come back for that later.

The specialist paramedic arrives quicker than I expected, interrupting the nail-biting conversation

I'm having with the patient about where he got his scarf from. It makes light conversation.

"He's not on Entonox?" The specialist paramedic comments.

"No, he refused any analgesia as he denies any pain."

My colleague looks back at me bewildered, as if to say 'one of you is lying'.

"You drunk?" He questions the patient.

"No, I don't drink"

"Something doesn't add up here" my colleague whispers into my ear.

When we eventually come up with a plan on how the two of us are going to get the patient onto our stretcher and into the ambulance, the patient agrees to Entonox just in case - highly likely - he feels any pain whilst we mobilise him. He quickly bleeds the Entonox dry before we move a muscle though. As my colleague supports the patient's good shoulder, I instruct the him to put all his weight into his good leg in an attempt to stand, whilst I support his dislocated leg. To our amazement though, his boot which was hanging off his foot to make it look like it was dislocated, comes flying off and his two structurally sound legs and ankles weight bear perfectly, without even as much as a wince. When he sees the look on my colleagues face though, both his legs suddenly become completely powerless for no apparent reason, and he throws himself onto our stretcher, landing right on his 'dislocated' shoulder, seemingly painlessly. We say nothing.

"Let's see that hip and shoulder then shall we?" My colleague questions when we're all secured on the ambulance.

"Sure, but I think everything is back in place now," he mumbles hesitantly.

"Nonsense!" Replies the specialist paramedic whilst helping the patient take off his jumper.

"I doubt it would be 'back in place' without any intervention, let's have a look"

I stand watching mortified, I can't believe I actually fell for this.

"What's that?" I suddenly question when I see another cashmere scarf, this one wrapped around his femur underneath his trouser leg.

"I put it on like a tourniquet, I thought it might help."

"Are you bleeding?"

"No it's for the dislocation."

My colleague and I look at one another not knowing whether to laugh or cry before he questions the patient further:

"Do you want to tell me why you carry two scarves mate? Or how you tied that scarf around your leg with a dislocated shoulder?"

"Umm… oh, well I…."

"It's a bit of a coincidence your house is just there," my crew mate continues whilst pointing out of the window. "And you were nice and toasty warm when my colleague finally found you out on the road she'd already checked three times with no sign of you, don't you think? Did you leave your house when you saw my colleague out there looking for you? Then you put your shoe on awkwardly to make it look like you dislocated your ankle?"

The patient is silent.

"Tell me you didn't drain all our Entonox despite not having an injured bone in your body? Go on, tell me?"

"Fine! I lied, there's nothing wrong with me. But what are you going to do about it?"

"No worries bud!" my colleague replies, putting emphasis on the word 'bud'. "We'll take you home to your parents and tell them of the stressful night you've had. They can look after you from there."

With that the patient darts out the back of the ambulance, quicker than I ever could, and leaves his scarf behind. Which apparently can also be used as a tourniquet, although there's no medical benefit in using one for a dislocation. Oh how I want to ring his doorbell and hand his scarf to his parents, but I don't. I leave it on his doorstep and hop back in my car before I change my mind.

"I'm so sorry," I apologise to the specialist paramedic, mortified.

"Not your fault. You couldn't assess him properly out there in the cold, you did exactly what I would have done in your situation. Let's just hope we scared him enough in threatening to involve his parents, the bell end doesn't do it again."

The specialist paramedic retired soon after this job. I don't think this patient had anything to do with it though... I hope not anyway.

CHAPTER FOURTY ONE:
System Error

We're literally in the middle of nowhere -again- and my patient is having a stonking STEMI that needs PPCI, or thrombolysis* immediately. And judging by his ECG, he is likely to go into a rhythm incompatible with life if he doesn't get treatment rapidly.

I begin the usual cocktail of drugs whilst my colleague attempts to get hold of Control to request HEMS. We're well over an hour away from emergency intervention in any direction, and I'm honestly not sure he will last that long judging by his abnormal vital signs and worsening coronary artery occlusion.

HEMS can either thrombolyse on scene, or get him to PPCI a hell of a lot quicker than we can. After ten minutes waiting though, I make the decision to just get going. For some unknown and rare reason, Control simply aren't answering their radio, and we can't just watch this man die in front of our eyes. Besides, HEMS might not even be available to help.

As we quickly mobilise the patient onto the ambulance, I ask his wife to travel in the front cab with the ECA. If he does arrest on me, I certainly don't want her witnessing the whole event, becoming understandably hysterical whilst I brutally attempt to restart his heart. A resus is by no means glamorous or heroic. I think if relatives saw us breaking their loved one's ribs, inflating them like a balloon and electrocuting them, then more would be less inclined to disagree with a 'do not resuscitate' - where appropriate.

We get going immediately on blue lights, as our satnav anticipates it taking an hour and ten minutes. We might get that down to half that on blues if we're lucky, but even thirty five minutes seems too slow for this time critical patient. Without delay I send the ECG to the receiving hospital and wait for a reply, but after five minutes when they haven't even read the message, I become concerned. Why aren't they replying? We're less than half an hour away now and he should really be going straight up to theatre. Someone is usually watching this emergency line waiting for this very occasion. It's very rare I've waited over thirty seconds before, so after resending again, it I decide to call them.

"Hello switchboard, how can I help?" That's very strange, I thought I had the direct number for PPCI, it shouldn't have put me through to switchboard, oh well, the kind voice at the end of the phone sounds like she should be able to help me.

"Oh hi there, I'm Georgia, a paramedic, would it be possible to put me through to PPCI regarding one of my patients please.

"... Umm I think you have the wrong number, I've never heard of PPCI" says the call handler. I pause for a second in dismay.

"...PPCI, you know percutaneous coronary intervention, or the coronary care unit (CCU)...

Where patients having heart attacks get a stent fitted."

"Oh no we certainly don't deal with that here love!"

"Sorry, have I got the wrong number?"

"I'm not sure dear, let me go and find out if we can help you."

When she still has me on hold five minutes later and we're only twenty five minutes from hospital I get frustrated and put the phone down before immediately ringing her back.

"Hello switchboard"

"Hello, its Georgia again. Could you just put me through to CCU please?"

"Oh yes, I spoke with my colleague and I don't think we're allowed to put you straight through to CCU, that's where our patients are awaiting treatment for a heart attack you know? I'll put you through to the ED."

I don't have time to argue that I'm well aware CCU is where heart attacks are treated! So I utter a thank you in the hope ED can put me directly through to CCU when I explain the situation. And thankfully they do without hesitation.

"Oh hello, I'm a paramedic and I have a patient in my ambulance having a STEMI. I've tried sending you their ECG but it doesn't seem to have gone through…"

"Can I just stop you there?" They interrupt. "You need to speak with PPCI, here, I'll give you their direct phone number."

"Thank you so much," I say relieved, but probably sounding more sarcastic.

"Hello, is this PPCI?"

"Yes, who is this?"

"Oh thank goodness, I'm a paramedic and have a patient for you, it won't let me send you the ECG for some reason, so can I just give you the story, my findings and our estimated time of arrival (ETA) over the phone?"

"Oh not again! Our computer has done this once before. The whole system goes down and nobody seems to be able to contact us, it'll be up and running in a moment to send us the ECG, but yes please, tell us the history in the mean time."

Just as I begin telling the nurse the history my radio goes off, its Control finally getting back to us. They can wait for me now, I'm in the middle of a handover I've been trying to give for nearly twenty minutes, and nothing is going to stop me from giving it. As we arrive through the heavy double doors at CCU after we tell Control they're no longer required, and the satnav packing up on us, I couldn't be more relieved to see numerous clinicians awaiting our arrival. They lead us straight into theatre with our patient, apologising profusely for the system error, whilst asking for another quick history before they insert a catheter into the patient's groin.

He made it! I'm overjoyed, and it must be written all over my face as a nurse who is a complete stranger to me, smiles whilst tapping me on the shoulder saying:

"You did good".

I honestly thought he was going to arrest on me whilst being conveyed to hospital, and after silently tearing my hair out on the phone and Control not getting back to me, I thought I might have a coronary myself! I'm instructed by PPCI to put in a datix for them about the situation, to prevent this situation from ever happening again. So when I get back to station an hour and a half after my finish time, I quickly put in my first ever datix.

CHAPTER FOURTY TWO:

Skiing

I was having the best week skiing, I can't believe I've never done it before being that I love the outdoors, adrenaline sports and the mountains more than anything; and I'm actually quite good at it. I never excelled at school, Cs across the board, pretty average. But skiing, I think I found my feet, with three lessons on a dry slope and five days into my holiday, I was parallel skiing down reds without a single fall and even getting myself down some black runs. So on the last day in Bansko before flying home, after completing the entire piste map, I had the day all planned in my head what we would do; basically redo all our favourites.

So we get to the first easy blue slope via the ski lift, which we are obliged to get down to get to the harder slopes that we so badly want to do - like children at a theme park. It's packed with beginners and still so icy at this time in the morning, but I'm an expert now, right? So I quickly race down, carving between hundreds of children, ski schools and experts, when all of a sudden I hit some ice mid turn and fall hard onto both hands in an attempt to protect my face, my legs spread, almost doing the splits and my ski's carrying on solo down the hill. No biggie, I've fallen many times, especially earlier in the week. However, this time I notice a sudden shearing pain in my wrist, but again, no big deal, every time I've fallen this week I've rolled around in pain for a second, before realising the pain quickly subsided and I got up to continue skiing down the mountain, uninjured. I'm not scared of falling. Therefore, it comes as no surprise that when people start rushing over to me to check I'm ok, 'A' tells them I'm fine and to carry on skiing past me. I roll around in pain for a while, but the pain doesn't ease this time. I roll around some more and the pain intensifies. I'm now lying in the middle of the busy ski slope crying and swearing in agony, I've never felt pain like this before.

'A' finally realises I'm injured and assists me to the side of the mountain. This is surprisingly a lot more difficult than I had anticipated, as every movement in an attempt to stand on ice causes an agonising shearing sensation going all the way up my arm. I feel really guilty now, as I recently told a football player with a very similar injury that I wouldn't drive the ambulance twenty feet across the pitch to him as there was nothing wrong with his legs.

Very quickly, mountain rescue come speeding up the piste on a skidoo to get me off the slope. I don't know who called them, but I'm very appreciative to whoever did so. They ask me if I want analgesia and I very quickly say:

"Yes please! Do you have morphine?"

They laugh and joke "No, how about cocaine?" Before they start talking and laughing in Bulgarian. It would have been funny if cocaine was even in the same category as an opioid*, but it's not. I realise I must have looked like a twat though and they thought exactly what I think when a patient asks me for morphine straight out the vial! So I reassure mountain rescue, I'm not a junkie, just a paramedic and I'm genuinely in a lot of pain. Turns out they don't carry morphine, just poxy tramadol, but I'll take what I can get. Besides, tramadol is a derivative of morphine after all. I forget sometimes that we're in a very unique position in the UK carrying basic paracetamol or morphine, with no interim.

The skidoo ride would have been much more fun if I wasn't in so much pain. Every mogul and break caused an excruciating shooting pain in my right arm and wrist. I was clinging on to the skidoo with my left hand, praying to God I wouldn't fall off going around left hand bends, fast.

To my delight, 'A' was waiting for me at the top of the gondola, a twenty minute ride away from the hospital at the base of the mountain.

Once we were finally sat in the waiting room of the hospital together the pain eased in my wrist a little, as it had been splinted and the tramadol was starting to take effect, but little did I know this would be so short lived. 'A' was amazing, ringing the insurance company and liaising with the Bulgarian medical team, as he wasn't allowed in the consultation room with me. I'm not used to being the patient, and I found out I don't make a very good one either. First they took off my ski jacket, gloves, base layer and jumper. So many layers. I ask them to just cut my jacket off which is what I usually do on the ambulance when the patient is in too much pain and agrees, but they just laugh -again- and get all my layers off effectively, but brutally, without shearing them to pieces. All be it in a spacious, well lit room I've just calmly walked into, as opposed to our confined ambulance. As soon as I see my wrist I know exactly what I've done, it's called a Colle's fracture, AKA swan neck or dinner fork fracture, as the wrist quite literally looks deformed like a swans neck or dinner fork. It's a complete fracture and dislocation of the distal radius* which may or may not involve a fracture to the distal ulna*. Before I go for x-ray I ask:

"It's a Colle's fracture isn't it?"

They all stop and look at me surprised and slightly concerned.

"Are you a doctor?" One of them asks.

"No, a paramedic." I reply.

"Same difference" he adds. No it's really not! But I smile for a second in receiving the compliment.

This is one of the only times they are even remotely pleasant to me and speak in English. Following a painful x-ray, the consultant confirms my suspicions and abruptly informs me in broken English to lie on the hard metal bed, where he's going to inject a local anaesthetic in my joint before performing a conscious closed reduction: manipulating the bones back into place, by pulling on my hand and pushing his knuckles into my deformed wrist. I ask if 'A' can come in with me now, I've heard how painful these can be. I panic when they say no. I plead, but the consultant still refuses and is getting irate now, so I do as he says, shut up and lie on the metal table with my eyes tightly squeezed. Tears start rolling down my already red wet cheeks as they inject the local anaesthetic into my wrist, I know what's coming, but I didn't think it would be so soon. The injection into the joint was painful enough, but before they give it any time to take effect, they pull on my joint in an attempt to relocate the bone. I scream the hospital down, I've never felt pain like this before, this was truly ten out of ten on any pain score. He's still pulling and digging his thumbs hard into my broken bones minutes later. Instinctively, I start thrashing my legs, forgetting I still have ski boots on. It makes a horrific sound and the bed jolts for a second with the force, but I can't help it, its utter agony. I really do make the worst patient. The doctor keeps looking at me as if to say 'what on earth is wrong with you?' And keeps laughing to his colleagues, speaking in Bulgarian. I don't even give a shit anymore though whether they're polite to me or not, I just want 'A', and I want all this to be over very quickly.

Finally, it ends, and I am re x-rayed to check if it's back in place. Thank the Lord it is, they would have had to put me to sleep if they wanted to do that again. Finally, they cast it, but in doing so, the doctor places his gigantic palms around my wrist and squeezes the cast directly to my skin as hard as he can to set it, as if squeezing an icing bag onto a cake. I wince in pain and cry yet again, the doctor very unsympathetic now. Finally, the ordeal is over,

I walk out to 'A' red faced and bleary eyed, and can't stop crying with relief when he hugs me. He's sorted all the insurance out so we can now leave. Before going back to the hotel, I practically run to the nearest pharmacy in my ski boots to get my hands on any analgesia they're willing to give me, I couldn't care less how much they charge me.

In all fairness, for an impoverished, under-developed country, they have done amazing. From the time of injury to the time of casting, it must have been no more than an hour, so we head back at the hotel by lunchtime. Now what to do with the rest of our valentine's day?

CHAPTER FORTY THREE:

Surgery

Today was the day of my operation. It's been two weeks since I fractured my wrist, and I only found out I needed surgery on it yesterday, my birthday. My birthday was all planned. I would go to the fracture clinic with a friend for another x-ray, then we'd go shopping together, before she'd drop me off at a beauty salon to have a massage and my nails shellacked. The last x-ray in the UK a week prior, showed a stable fracture, which just required six weeks in a cast.

We are not allowed painted nails in the ambulance service, so I figured if I'm going to be off work for another six weeks, then I'll treat myself. Finally, when 'A' arrived home from work, he was going to be taking me out for a surprise meal. It was perfect, considering I couldn't climb, which I'd normally do on my birthday.

I had woken up that morning, surprised to see a gift at the side of the bed that 'A' had left for me, as he bought me a pet rabbit yesterday for my birthday present, and I thought that was all I was getting. Excitedly I opened my present and hopped out of bed ready to attend my early fracture clinic appointment. I wasn't at all concerned, as last week's x-ray showed a successful closed reduction in Bulgaria, so no need for an operation; they just needed to confirm it weekly. As my friend headed to the shops - where I would meet her in no more than thirty minutes I thought - I had my x-ray. As soon as the doctor called me in to the consultation room and I saw the x-rays on a large television screen though, my heart sank. It didn't take a medically trained professional to see that the bone wasn't where it was supposed to be.

"Oh fuck!" I accidently said out loud.

"Try not to worry, we have some options," the doctor explained.

He proceeded to inform me I have a choice. I can either leave it be, let it heal in this deformed way, but never be able to write properly with my right hand again, let alone climb or drive an ambulance. Or have another relocation with wires inserted via general anaesthetic to hold the bone in place whilst it heals, which will then be removed at a later date. It was a no brainer. They could have amputated my arm and stitched it back together three times for all I cared, so long as I could climb and work again, that's all that mattered.

"Great, we'll get you in tomorrow."

"Tomorrow?!" I replied.

"Yes, it needs to be relocated as soon as possible to prevent it from healing in a deformed position" he continued.

I'd never had surgery before, I was nervous but excitedly curious. I rung 'A' at work, who just so happened to be on route to the same hospital with a patient, so once he handed them over in ED, he came to see me for a quick coffee. We discussed whether we should go out for my surprise meal. I pleaded with him that we still go, I could still eat before midnight then not consume anything afterwards, as instructed. He put his head down.

"I'm going to have to tell you where were going now, it's the cheese and wine bar, you can eat cheese, but you can't drink, so there really is no point". He was right, I certainly couldn't drink my body weight in wine before I had surgery the next day. There goes that then, I thought.

Just as 'A' left to go back to work and I got ready to head to the shops, I received a phone call telling me to head up to the day surgery ward for my pre-surgery
assessment.

"How long do you think this will take?" I asked when I arrived.

"Between one and three hours" a voice staring down and shuffling sheets of paper informed me. Three hours! My beautician appointment was in two and a half. I sat down to read the numerous pieces of paperwork they asked me to scroll through, and the first thing it said was no alcohol, and no nail varnish or jewellery. So I cancelled my beautician appointment and informed my friend I might be a little longer than expected. Eventually, a health care assistant called me in to help me fill in the paperwork and take my blood pressure - as I can't write currently, and if I try, it looks like I'm either four years old or have the IQ of a jellyfish.

"Put your coat over there" she instructed, as we walked into a cubicle and she pointed to the corner with only a drip stand in it.

Without thinking, I hung my coat over the inexpensive piece of equipment and took a seat. She asked ridiculous questions, like how likely are you to fall asleep whilst driving, and have you ever suffered gout? Before weighing and measuring me. I still have no idea why gout would be remotely relevant. Then she just stopped, mid-sentence, still as a post, for about ten seconds.

"Sorry, I'm going to have to measure that again, I was just so unbelievably shocked that you'd hang your coat on our equipment." She retorted, with a disapproving voice.

I laughed, but her face soon told me she wasn't joking, so I quickly removed my coat from the drip stand silently. Eventually when we were both sat down again, she started questioning me further, and when it got to my occupation, she was not impressed.

"You're a paramedic and you hung your coat on our equipment, you should know better young lady." She snapped.

I wanted to say 'it's just a drip stand and a lightweight coat you old bat.' But instead I stayed silent and tried not to laugh; or cry. Eventually I was allowed to leave and I tried enjoying what was left of my birthday.

***

This morning I awoke very full from last night's Italian, and surprisingly eager for my operation. I hate having a broken wrist, but if I'm going to have one, why not get all the sympathy of an operation and morphine? But I think that makes me a bad person for even considering that, so I try and think differently. This was the first time I was going to have morphine, and judging by previous patients' reactions, I couldn't wait. We arrive bright and early, as there was no traffic on the road at that time in the morning, and perch ourselves against a wall in the waiting room as it's so busy. But, just as I go to tell 'A' I think we're going to be here a while, they call my name. 'A' is asked to leave and to pick me up this afternoon.

"Can he not be there when I wake up?" I ask.

"No, visitors aren't allowed in the day surgery ward, only to drop off and pick up." They reply. So 'A' leaves. He took the day off work for me, I feel awful now, but he reassures me he'll get loads of studying done and change the tyres on my car before my MOT whilst he's in the area.

Soon after he leaves, the orthopaedic surgeon who explained the options to me yesterday comes down and explains my procedure, followed by the anaesthetist - who I recognise from my week's theatre placement at university. Both treat me with the upmost respect and talk to me in medical jargon - some of it I understand - and laugh that I have a medical textbook to read during the waiting times. I hope I didn't seem pretentious, I didn't even think about it until then, I just enjoy reading, there's always more to learn.

I don't even get a full page into my book though when a nurse comes to collect me to inform me they're ready for me in theatre. I must be the first one. That was lucky. As they wheel me on the hospital bed, I recognise the corridors leading into operating theatres and the recovery room. It was here I intubated my first patient, and watched a full hip replacement, live. I don't normally get squeamish, but that hip replacement was just something else. I think any brick layer could potentially be an orthopaedic surgeon judging by the tools the clinicians use replicating bolsters and power drills, and how they utilise them to put stubborn, solid bones back together. As they wheel my bed into the anaesthetists cubicle* I am calm and relaxed. I've seen this done to many patients and I trust the anaesthetist wholeheartedly - I should do, he breathes for me during the entire operation! I don't even notice them cannulate me and inject profolol* into my veins, as I'm so engrossed in conversation with the anaesthetist about how I'd love to do his job - the morphine had kicked in. The room started going up and down quickly, and there were suddenly three anaesthetists that all looked identical, but I wasn't scared, I felt surprisingly calm, like in a trance. I think I must have fallen asleep mid-sentence as I don't ever remember finishing my conversation when I woke up. I don't even remember waking up, I just remember talking to the nurse, asking him how long he's been a nurse for now.

"That's the third time you've asked me that" he laughs.

"What are you talking about, I've only been awake a few minutes".

"No, we've been sat here talking for nearly an hour".

An hour?! What had I been talking about for an hour? I could have said literally anything and I would have been none the wiser. I can only liken it to being drunk, but even then, I've never had amnesia whilst intoxicated, although many people do.

I feel strangely euphoric when they take me back to the ward. The sun is shining, everything looks brighter and tastier and sounds are more intensified, I feel fantastic.

"Can I go home now?" I ask the sister in charge.

"No not yet." She laughs. "You've only just come back from the recovery room and we need to monitor you for at least two hours."

"Fair enough, but I feel fine, ready to run a marathon in fact."

I'm given tea and toast, but am not allowed to get dressed yet, so when I make my way to the toilet without a care in the world, thinking how lovely this life is, a nurse comes hurrying over to me to tell me my gown is undone at the back and I'm showing the ward everything.

"Oh, am I?" I say calmly, without a giving a damn.

Less than an hour later, they agree I'm probably fine, and ring 'A' to come pick me up. He's so good.

"Are you in any pain in your wrist?" The nurse asks me before I leave.

Oh my wrist, I totally forgot about that. I look down and see my arm in a colossal bandage wrapped around a monumental plaster cast in a sling. My hair all tangled up in the sling- I love having long hair, until these things happen.

"No. I think I'm ok" I reply. And we leave.

It's only this evening I feel like death. My wrist is making crunching noises and grinding every time I move my arm, its agony, and despite sleeping all afternoon, I just can't keep my eyes open, yet my body won't let me sleep. Tired but wired. 'A' looks at me and laughs:

"You do look like you've just had an anaesthetic".

CHAPTER FOURTY FOUR:
Covid 19

I've been cooped up for months and months with this wrist fracture, just as Covid-19 has taken hold. I've self isolated for eight weeks, and that had nothing to do with the corona virus. I just simply couldn't drive or ride my bike, or even carry the shopping home due to my wrist. Yet somehow, I still developed a cough and a temperature at one point. 'A' said I'll have to self isolate, and I laughed telling him my life won't change one bit for the week. His did though, I think he enjoyed his two weeks off work whilst I had a temperature of 37.9.

Everyone had been telling me I couldn't have chosen a better time to break a bone and be off work, its mayhem, they wish they were at home, but I couldn't disagree more. The world had never needed people like me so much, and I was lounging about the house, helpless and disabled, getting bored out my brain. I just wanted to be out there making a difference, doing exactly what I was trained for. But instead I was just sat at home, yearning to get my cast off and start driving, no matter the pain.

I'll be the first to admit I thought Covid was a load of over exaggerated bollox to begin with. I'd have lengthy telephone conversations with my paramedic friends on how ridiculous this all is and what a crazy world we live in.

"We've had so much worse." I'd tell them, "HIV, swine flu, measles, foot and mouth". The list went on. But then one day it hit my tiny cynical brain. Until that point I had only read about elderly and severely disabled patients dying. 'Just as many die of the common cold when they're that frail or low in immunity' I thought. But I was so wrong. A tri-athlete was being interviewed on the news and he explained how he was ventilated in intensive care. He was young, ran marathons, had no underlining co-morbidities and very nearly died from the confirmed corona virus. Although he was on the mend, he could no longer walk up the stairs without becoming breathless, let alone run his usual weekly marathon. This hit me hard. I like to think of myself as quite fit, I always push my limits in climbing to become the best I possibly can. At least I did when I had the use of two wrists. I'm just getting into triathlons and I've signed myself up to a number of half marathon races this summer. But I'm by no means an iron man tri-athlete, running marathons on my days off, or swimming across oceans. If this man had been in intensive care, what hope have the rest of us got? I became terrified, but in doing so I finally learnt how I would like to live for the rest of my life. I would ring my mum and sisters on facetime every day and we'd talk for hours. I'd never facetimed my mum before. Then when I got off the phone, I'd ring my dad for exactly the same situation. 'A' and I spent quality time together during our self isolation. We'd play along with *Catchphrase* and drink wine before having coffee in bed the next morning and make ourselves lemon drizzle and salted caramel cakes. Isn't this the life everybody dreams of? If I could continue this life when Covid is over, but also see friends, climb and work at the same time, I think I would have truly found the meaning of happiness.

***

Today though is my first day back at work, and covid is far from over! There have only been ten thousand confirmed cases in the UK, but the government expect the fatalities to reach over twenty thousand. The war has only just begun. As I drive down the deserted high street to do my bit for society, I'm astounded by what I see. I knew there would be very few cars on the roads, unnecessary shops would not be open for business, precincts would be closed and holidays would be postponed. We've had to postpone two of our own climbing holidays, partly due to Covid and partly my wrist. But to actually see this in real life is just something else. I promise to myself to never forget this time and to be forever grateful for what I have. People weren't exaggerating when they said it was like a zombie apocalypse out there, I've never felt more like an actress in a film in all my life. Not a single runner, or shopper or car, just me, and the wind blowing the month old rubbish down the street. Nobody ever expected this to actually be real life. Am I in a dream? I'd quite like to be woken up now and continue my ordinary wonderful life.

As I pull into the ambulance station I couldn't be more relieved to find cars parked outside and the silhouettes of bodies moving around upstairs through the windows. All be it fewer cars than usual and the bodies were frantically running here there and everywhere, but I'm no longer alone in this world.

I'm not back on the front line yet, I can barely drive my car in my splint, let alone a heavy ambulance on blue lights! More to the point, I can't perform CPR or even imagine lifting the carry chair with even the lightest of patients on it. A paramedic who can't drive or perform CPR is laughable, so I'm put on light duties.

I've been told not to put any weight through my wrist for the next three months, so even light duties is frustratingly difficult. Whilst I slowly write the dates on drugs bags, I'm careful to ensure they're legible with my left handwriting, and have to continue taking co-codamol four hourly whilst at work, for all the typing I'm doing on the computer, completing plaudits and writing never ending emails. I could never hold down an office job in the past, I had to be out there in the community, making a difference, with no day ever being the same. But we've all had to make sacrifices during this unmanageable time, I hardly think sitting at a computer desk on full pay is the worst situation I could be in right now! I am so jealous of my colleagues though, as they come back to the station for their lunches telling stories of their action packed days. They explain how the last three patients they've been to have probably all had Covid, but are either not severe enough for ICU, or refuse hospital, as they know they will likely never see their family again, and would likely die alone due to no visitors being allowed, under any circumstances.

"Our last patient will be dead in a week I imagine" says one of the paramedics bluntly. But what can any of us do? Other clinicians come back gasping for water from where they've performed a full resuscitation attempt in heavy aprons, masks and goggles in the hot weather. If any patient is unconscious, paramedics' are required to be fully 'suited and booted', as the patient cannot tell you if they've had any symptoms. I don't think it will be long before we have to wear PPE to all patients, symptoms or no symptoms. I haven't heard one clinician talk about any patient who has rung for anything other than Covid yet. I'm frightened for the stroke patients and the heart attacks that will inevitably still occur, no matter what the world's current situation. With less than half the usual staff at work due to furlough and mild fevers, and patients with a slight coughing episode ringing up here there and everywhere as a result of pure fear, who is going to attend the other time critical patients?

The whole thing is utter mayhem, but thanks to every single key worker on our planet, its organised mayhem. This isn't a war against each other, it's the entire world coming together in a fight for life.

CHAPTER FOURTY FIVE:
Narcan

Its been three months almost to the day since my last uneventful twelve hour shift. At the time I was wrongly completely disinterested in listening to other peoples bull shit, faking a smile whilst I fantasised about being on the side of a mountain only two days in the future, parallel skiing down some black, almost ninety degree slope, like some wonder woman. Of course this never happened; particularly as it was my first time skiing. I wish I was as talented as my imagination and fantasies make out! I finished that shift an hour late, trying desperately not to think about my next shift in only twelve days time. Little did I know that I wouldn't actually be back on an ambulance in twelve days at all, but more like twelve weeks. A tedious, unimaginably boring, relentless ninety days, of over thinking and de-skilling.

I wish I could go back to that day three months ago and tell the old me, who was blind, to enjoy that shift. To take in every single moment and realise how far she's come, because I haven't been, nor will I be that confident again in a long time; after the longest time I've ever spent away from an ambulance in four years. I dread to think if I ever go off on maternity leave. I laugh for a second though as I pause and think to myself, I could tell her to enjoy that shift as much as I damn well please. It still won't change where I am or how I feel today. But at least I would have been more appreciative of my average but brilliant life.

Today is my first day back on the frontline and I'm more nervous than ever. My first day as a paramedic was a breeze compared to this. And my first day a student paramedic. Laughable! What I would do now to have a mentor. Or a preceptorship week. No, this time it's just me, all on my own, and the expectations are high. I've been registered well over a year now, so I should know exactly what I'm doing. 'Should' being the operative word. But I've hardly left the house in weeks since my accident, let alone stepped foot on an ambulance as the most senior clinician. And covid is spreading like the plaque. Patients dropping like flies here, there, and everywhere, and I don't have the equipment to protect them. Or myself.

I was fitted for an FFP3 mask*, but just like over 50% of my colleagues, it doesn't fit adequately. When I was tested, both the synthetic, manmade sweet and bitter fragranced particles made their way through the tiny seems in my mask, up my nose and into the back of my throat, making my eyes water and gag. Did they accidently put tear gas in mine? If these atoms can reach my respiratory tract through a tightly fitted suffocating mask, leaving a temporary scar around my nose and chin, then unscented, tasteless covid particles most definitely could, undetected until its too late, and I've infected at least half of my patients. Many of whom will most likely being immunocompromised*. With FFP3 masks not being a viable option for the shape if my face (although I'm still unsure why since I blatantly – I really really hope blatantly- don't have a beard), my only option for aerosol generating procedures* (AGPs), cardiac arrests and unresponsive patients, is a powered hood. And wearing this whilst trying to perform CPR or run an arrest is like sprinting a marathon, in a sauna suit, in the desert. I'd imagine.

For the rest of the population ringing 999 though, who are very much alive and conscious and are breathing adequately without requiring any AGPs. Well they're just as fucked as I am, since we're dangerously low on face masks, and have been informed to use them 'sparingly'. Whatever that means?

Despite uncertainty, anxiety and utter confusion though, I really am trying to do my very upmost to protect myself, my colleagues and my patients. Doing everything parliament is telling me to do, because they must know what they're talking about. Right?

I have a cleverly designed handmade washbag made from a pillowcase to put my used uniform in after each and every shift, ready to go straight into the wash on the highest temperature setting. And I'm stocked up on as many masks, aprons and gloves as I think I might need for one twelve hour shift.

Although I don't know what 'sparingly' actually really means in this situation, I'm absolutely certain it's still an obvious requirement to change masks between patients, and we've not actually run out of masks yet, so I'm not putting my patients at risk. Especially when that risk is death! If I don't wear a mask to a patient who is later found out to have had asymptomatic covid, 'just in case' the government run out, and actually we never run out of masks at all, as predicted (or even if we do!), I don't have a leg to stand on! Professionally or myself mentally. So the masks keep going on until I'm specifically told otherwise. For most patients, the flimsy, thin piece of material allowing air to flow in and out of our lungs -all be it reduced- is the only barrier we have, between potentially catching a highly contagious, life ending, orphan and widow making virus. Please don't take that away from us too Boris.

As well as taking precautions whilst on shift though, it's also so vital I remind myself there really is no point if I'm going to be a dick at home. Of course, I'm absolutely desperately yearning to go to my local beach on my days off, or climb on the cliffs at my local crag, along with all the other furloughed irresponsible teenagers, parents and flat earthers! Albeit climb pathetically with my weak wrist, which is half the size of the other since it's come out its cast, due to muscle wastage. But I have a duty. A responsibility. Not as a professional or an NHS provider -although I definitely have that too. But as a human being. Just like we all do. Whilst my colleagues witness death, almost daily now; cancer patients have to wait longer for their life saving treatment; students are paying nine grand a year on attending university when they can't actually 'attend' university, and fragile dementia patients in nursing homes think their loved ones have forgotten about them because their failing minds can't recollect or comprehend covid exists, can I really justify going for a picnic in the park? Or desperately looking for a car parking space in an overcrowded, over filled car park full of thousands of cars already, so I can sit on an overpopulated piece of grass or sand, just inches away from a stranger, due to there simply not being enough land to sit any further away? Even though I'm outside. No, I cant. So when I drive home from work, I go straight home. I don't stop for a drink with a friend, or a barbequed burger with my sister. I go straight home, with a sore face from wearing a mask all day, and get ready for my next shift. Mostly by trying to sleep, but even that's a challenge when I'm filled with utter terror and uncertainty.

I wonder what my neighbours think of me on my days off, when they see I haven't left my house or garden in days, unless I have my uniform in my clinical, freshly washed work bag.

Maybe they think I'm a recluse and I choose not to go out? Maybe they think I genuinely don't want to see my best friend desperately, even just for a coffee. Like I'm not as deserving as them, or don't care as much as them? I mean they must think that right? To clap every Thursday evening for me, for 'A' and my thousands of colleagues working tirelessly, before going back into their occupied houses and continuing their house parties and social gatherings?

Either way, I don't think they've considered the fear I'm feeling as I 'suit up' in my tyvek coveralls*, ready for my first call out in months. And my first call out is a cardiac arrest. Fucking fantastic!

On route I discuss with my experienced ECA how this even works. Do we both 'suit and boot' when we arrive then go in together? And if so, do we do that outside the patient's house whilst they anxiously wait for our arrival? Watching their loved one seemingly wither away, whilst they witness us ponce about putting arms carefully in sleeves trying not to rip them, before putting what looks like a rocket helmet on our heads as if we're landing in one of the moons craters, which just so happens to be filled with acid -and not the good kind, I imagine. Or do we suit up before even leaving station?

Turns out that what this ECA has currently been doing, is the least qualified of the two of us enters the patient's house, solely in an apron, gloves and a generic, universal mask to establish whether one: it really is an arrest, as many times information can be misinterpreted or relayed wrong. And two; to establish whether the arrest is actually workable, or if efforts would be futile.

If the patient is for resuscitation, the plan remains, and the second clinician continues changing into the full personal protective equipment (PPE) required, whilst the ECA performs basic life support (BLS)*. Once kitted up, the fully kitted paramedic can then take over BLS, whilst the ECA goes to the ambulance to kit up themselves. Only once the ECA returns, can advanced life support (ALS)* commence. Of course, BLS usually involves necessary oxygenation as well as chest compressions and defibrillation. But in these unprecedented times, oxygenating a deceased patient -or a conscious patient for that matter- is an aerosol generating procedure. This means it's not only unsafe, but also goes against every guideline, to supply the patient with the vital oxygen they require in order to not potentially be left with a hypoxic brain injury, whilst we're in basic PPE.

And there's more. Another massive unimaginable difference currently, is that if a patient is found in asystole, and there's no obvious cause of death staring us right in the face, that's it. Efforts aren't attempted. The patient is pronounced dead. It's counterproductive to all my training. Ludicrous. It goes against everything I've ever been taught, and it's done nothing for my mental health, nor that of any of my colleagues, no matter how sound of mind we may have started.

We are of course taught this way of working when it comes to mass casualty, multi-trauma scenarios. Do the least for the most. More lives saved. And it works. But nobody actually ever expects to really have to utilise that training in UK ambulance world. Not really. Maybe at the beginning when you first learn it, but as the days turn into weeks and the weeks months and the months years, it becomes more and more unlikely and further and further from your mind. Only a year in and almost four years since I was taught the 'do the least for the most' phenomenon, and I hadn't even considered that this would ever even be an option. How naive was I?

As we pull up to the fifty one year olds flat, we do exactly what we plan. As the senior clinician, I remain in the truck and quickly but effectively slide into my PPE. A Tyvek suit over my uniform first, zipping it over every exposed piece of clothing, leaving only my boots, hands and head unprotected; going careful not to rip any holes in it as I go, which would send me back at square one. Second, I apply the powered hood, which will protect my eyes, face, and most importantly my airway, from coming into contact with the virus. I attach the hood to the fitted belt and turn the air conditioning on once its fully secure, but then realise I can't hear myself think, so turn it off until absolutely necessary. Finally, whilst thinking to myself I'm pleased I didn't try to become an astronaut, I attempt to apply gloves to my sweaty hands. If there's one thing I hate, its putting gloves on last, on damp, clammy fingers. Frustrating doesn't even touch it when they've ripped for a forth time! Once the gloves are finally applied over the suit with no rips, leaving no skin on show, I am ready to make my way to the front door, where the patient and ECA await my arrival.

As I approach the scene, I am surprised to see no CPR in progress. I assumed my colleague would have radioed me if full PPE wasn't required. After all it took over five minutes to get ready by the time I was on my fifth pair of gloves! As he turns to see me though, panicked, sweat dripping off his brow, I notice the patient lying comatose on their living room floor, albeit still breathing, but slowly. I think I'll require my full PPE after all. I immediately go to grab my stethoscope from my trouser pocket to help establish the cause of the bradypnoea*, although I already have a good idea what's causing it, judging by the full sharps boxes and loose needles in the apartment. Just as I do so though, I'm met with the thick pocketless tyvek suit. Shit! I've left my stethoscope in my uniform, secured beneath a layer protecting my green clothing. Just then the radio goes off. I go to answer it. 'Are you fucking kidding me?! I ask myself internally. That's attached to my trouser pocket also. My ECA see's my problem and laughs. Not for long though. Our patient's condition is declining, and we can't administer oxygen until we're both suited up!

As my colleague leaves the apartment, back up arrives. We haven't had chance to inform Control this isn't a cardiac arrest yet, so similarly to ourselves, one paramedic comes rushing in, in their full PPE whilst the other remains on the truck kitting up. Unlike us, the double paramedic crew agreed that the passenger would put on their PPE on route to scene. I'll think of that next time. I haven't got much if any of a history yet, but I handover all the information I have:

"We've only literally just arrived, but found this fifty one year old in bradypnea, GCS 6 on our arrival."

"I CANT HERE ANYTHING YOU'RE SAYNG" shouts my colleague, desperately switching all the buttons on the powered belt in an attempt to turn the noisy air conditioner off.

"LOOKS LIKE WE'RE GOING TO NEED NARCAN*." I bellow, pointing at the exposed needles.

"No need to shout" She sarcastically laughs, as she finally terminates the synthetic air forcing itself onto her face, and opens the drug bag to locate the particularly quick acting antidote reversing narcotics*.

Narcan is by far the quickest acting drug we carry, transforming comatose, apnoeic* patients with track marks* all the way up their arms, who are most certainly close to death, into delightful, unappreciative, fully alert, individuals in a matter of seconds. Whom of which are almost always more than ready for a fight after we just 'ruined' their hit they spent good money on. Even though we did just in effect, save their life.

The quick gasping for breath and sitting bolt upright before talking in full comprehendible sentences immediately after the administration of the drug, is one area of accuracy portrayed in many films and soap operas. Although it's not quite as common to jab the medication straight into a patient's sternum- or heart- with great force from about a meter over the patients chest, as some films suggest. And the medic definitely has their eyes wide open whilst they administer it. Not tightly squeezed in anticipation and fear- again, as some movies suggest.

"Oh, it's not an arrest then?" The third paramedic questions as she enters the scene fully suited up, with my crew mate close behind, and the patient wriggling and groaning just as we finish disposing of the intramuscular (IM) needle. He meets our expectations perfectly.

"Fuuuuuuuck" The patient squeals aggressively in anger. Red mist filling his bloodshot eye's. His anger quickly reverts to bewilderment though, and I'd even go as far as saying fear, when his eyes adjust to find four figures dressed up to the nines in what look like space suits, looking over what was his lifeless body. We do look like right plums.

His flat looks like it's been used as a drug den with teeming sharps boxes, uncapped needles attached to empty syringes, disused torniquets, rolled up twenty pound notes, credit cards and empty clip seal clear plastic bags. As well as the sporadic dried vomit, trashed china, furniture and glass bottles and numerous stained mattresses filling every corner. That's not to mention the pungent smell, suggesting an entire cannabis plant growing in the second bedroom.

Thankfully, we administered the lifesaving, quick acting medication through a disposable IM needle, leaving no port for the patient to self-administer heroin straight into his open vein, since he runs quicker down the stairs and down the high street, vanishing into the distance, faster than an exhilarated child on Christmas morning.

Not so thankfully however, the effects of opioids - which we know he's injected into himself now, since the medication worked- last a great deal longer than the quick half-life of Narcan. Meaning, in a few short hours, our patient will highly likely find himself in the same position he was when we initially pulled up on scene. Hopefully, with another 'caring' friend, who rings 999 for him when he becomes unresponsive. Even if the friend flees, leaving the patients front door wide open, prior to the ambulance -and police- arrival.

CHAPTER FOURTY SIX:
Are You Ready?

For our final call out on my first traumatic, hideous night shift back at work, we've been called to a labour. I'm excited but nervous. It's on my pathetic little bucket list to deliver a baby. Although when everything runs smoothly, they mostly deliver themselves, simply requiring a generic pair of hands to catch them as they plunge out off a very messy scene in one final push. And nobody ever wants to go to a labour that doesn't run smoothly. If there's anything at all that scares the shit out of any paramedic, no matter how well trained or experienced, it's a complicated labour.

I've witnessed babies being delivered by a variety of methods whilst on a maternity placement at university. But not witnessed, let alone delivered one myself on the road; metaphorically or literally. And so therefore, no, I've definitely not had a baby named after me. Unfortunately. And highly unlikely, even if I had have delivered the screaming pooping machine myself.

The first head I witnessed being brutally forced out of a bloody, but initially intact vagina, overstretching its diameter to that of a cantaloup melon (at least!), ripping its owner's perineum* in two, almost made me get a sex change! It was by no means the magical or life defining experience I had naively hoped for, I'm sorry to say. Especially after this messy, chaotic horror was the conclusion to a stop-start 72-hour labour, following an induction. And she still yet had to deliver the placenta, before being sutured at her most intricate, sensitive region, whilst salty water to clean her laceration stung her bare, torn anatomy. My old mentor told me watching his first child being born was like watching his favourite pub burn down, and for the first time, I could see his point entirely.

For a brief moment in time, caesareans seemed the only humane option. That was of course until I witnessed one. Perfect neat incisions, in a well lit wide open space, where the mother feels nothing for the entire process, and is handed her tiny miracle, unstressed, whilst an opaque screen allows the surgeons to tidy up any disarray. Leaving a well-ordered scar to delicately heal. Inconvenient at worst. Or so I thought.

In reality, what I actually witnessed scarred me for life. The most traumatic process I've ever witnessed, far above any thoracotomy* or open skull fracture. After some very precarious, unsympathetic incisions from the highly skilled and experienced surgeon, he looked his junior doctor right in the eye and uttered:

"Ready?"

"Ready" the lesser trained expert replied.

'Ready for what?' I thought, and with that I was quickly enlightened. At exactly the same time, both doctors put both their hands inside the unsuspecting lady's abdomen, clenching her torn bare skin, muscle and adipose tissue, and pulled, like they'd never pulled anything before. Apparently it heals better this way. I was astounded as I watched two high level clinicians play tug of war with the exposed peritoneum*, for literally minutes, whilst ripping, tearing sounds echoed through the surgical walls. After I thought I had witnessed everything, they clearly weren't pulling hard enough, because the less senior doctor put both of her feet on the metal rungs of the surgical bed, now putting her entire weight into the tugging. With one final large rip, they stopped, and wiped the sweat from their heads as they composed themselves. It didn't matter how calmly the baby was extracted from the uterus any longer, and how heart warming it was to hear that babies first cry; although that was a joyously stomach throbbing moment as a woman. My jaw was dropped, and it wasn't moving an inch.

I think what was most alarming to me, was the blissfully unaware mother, whose eyes gleamed with excitement and anticipation without so much as a flinch as she awaited her flesh and blood. Thankfully for her, not literally her flesh and blood!

By the forth and final labour of the week though, executed calmly, almost silently and plain right perfectly, by a woman I can only compare to wonder woman (but heavier with placenta and baby weight), delivering a little monster went back on my bucket list. Personally and professionally. Not like this though, not like I ever thought the next job would progress.

As the job comes through and the long awaited words ping up on the screen: 'labour', I almost jump for joy out of my seat.

"Yes!" I shout, eyes gleaming and grinning ear to ear. "I hope we get to deliver it!"

"I don't." My colleague replies bluntly, whilst screwing his face up and rubbing his weary eyes after a long night.

I've been to a few labours as a paramedic, but none have ever progressed quick enough for me to witness the end result. Well actually the penultimate result, as technically the delivery of the placenta is the end result, and my adrenaline juices and maternal instincts certainly aren't flowing for that. Each and every time though, the mother has been both more than happy and capable to walk into the maternity ward, and I wondered why they dialled 999, when they've had nine whole months to prepare for this very, unavoidable situation. But I happily transport them anyway. Just in case.

Just as I start to get excited though, we get an update. 'Gestation period* 16 weeks' its reads. Immediately my face takes a very different expression, and me and my ECA hope and pray it's a typing error. It isn't. As dread and guilt circle my veins, I can't help but wonder whether this should have ever even been coded a labour, as a foetus simply isn't viable at this stage of pregnancy, and will most likely be swallowed up in clots, endometrial tissue* and blood.

In deafening silence we progress to the scene, where we are met by a very calm mother, her two young children playing in the living room next door, and a not so collective grandmother. Our patient lays on her kitchen floor. Her back propped up with pillows whilst her legs are spread apart, concealed by a layer of towels, blankets, and incontinence pads. She shouts at her children to quieten down, before calmly apologising for the noise, whilst her mother frantically runs between the kitchen and the hallway, gathering her daughter's belongings for a hospital admission, in an emotional frenzy. Although the patient is covered well, its obvious to see the heart breaking truth that she has most likely lost her baby, due to the sheer amount of blood and uterine tissue staining her kitchen floor.

"It's ok, I know I've lost it" the expectant mother only a few short hours ago tells me when she sees the look on my face before I say a word. "I think he came out not so long ago." Although it was too early to tell the gender on a scan, she's convinced she was pregnant with a boy. Maybe wishful thinking after having two daughters, maybe a mother's instinct, maybe because miscarriages and still born's are most common in boys. Who knows. But right now she really didn't care what gender it was.

"It was most likely a large clot you passed" I try to reassure the patient "But it does look that way in that you've lost him. I really am so sorry for your loss." I attempt to sympathise. But there really is absolutely nothing I can say to ease even just a small ounce of her pain.

"Don't worry, I really am ok" the consultant obstetrician replies, whilst still laying in a pool of her own blood. Smiling at me like I don't have a clue. I don't.

"Is it ok if I remove some of these towels to see how much blood you've lost?"

"Of course"

In doing so I get a painful, unexpected shock. There before my eyes is something I've never witnessed before, never even comprehended I'd ever come across in my entire career.

It looks so unnatural, so inhuman, but at the same time it's one of the most upsetting sights I've ever witnessed because it is just so human. I have to dig deep to find the correct words. To find any words at all.

It takes the form of a baby boy in the foetal position, about the same size as my palm. He's purple in colour and almost entirely transparent. He's isn't yet fully developed, but he has two closed eyes, a protrusion where a nose would have formed, and a line for a mouth; reminiscent of a face. He has toes and fingers, but they are entirely webbed, and his arms are still attached firmly to his body. He's entirely comparable to one of those baby alien toys covered in makeshift slime and nestled in a plastic egg, often found in 90s kids party bags. He is completely still, to be expected. As am I.

Most people go to work and type emails, or answer the phone so they can pay their bills. I've come to work and seen a dead baby boy. What am I doing? I stare for a moment. I feel so many emotions all at once. Disturbed and unsettled, but also angry, confused, guilty and regretful. All whilst feeling empty in my gut. To my core. I feel my eyes filling. I must stop this right now! I do. I remind myself that this is not my life, this is not my baby, and I have to have more respect for this poor poor mother, her boy and her family. I am a professional and I have to act like one. I am not going through what this grieving mother is, not even close. Not even a little bit. It's the unimaginable for her.

I quickly switch off my emotions and return to my mentally robotic form, as I very gently place the towel back where it was. I almost lost it for a second there, and the look on the patient's face tells me she knows. She cannot see what I witnessed from the position she's laid in, but she can see me, and she can see her Mother, pale as a sheet, silent, still, with both her hands over her mouth behind me. I didn't cover the sight quickly enough. I gulp and ask the patient if she would like to see what her mother and myself just have. She refuses. So calmly and swiftly when the grandmother has taken herself to another room, I ever so gently place what I have found in numerous tissues so not to be seen, and carry it to the ambulance, as if I'm carrying the crown jewels- but even more carefully.

We drive back to station from the maternity unit in silence once more, whilst I wonder whether that was even the correct ward to transfer our patient. The thing, the foetus, the baby, the human, the life; it, him. I've no idea what name to use, or what to say, or even what emotions I'm entitled to feel anymore.

I wonder a whole array of questions. Whether this job will stay with me for the rest of my life. It will. Why it happened. Why it was me who got called to it and me who found the disturbing scene and not my ECA. Why did the mother not want to see her baby, no matter how undeveloped? Will he have a funeral? Almost definitely not. Should I feel guilty for feeling sad when it's not my baby? Should I feel guilty for even questioning that and my emotions when this is not about me? Should I be desperately trying to hide from my colleague as I wipe away a tear in the passenger seat of the cab as we pull into station?

***

It's only been twelve hours since I finished my last shift, and the first job of the night tonight is another maternity. What are the chances of that? Whilst early this morning I was almost jumping out my seat in excitement and anticipation at the thought of delivering a healthy new-born full term baby, this evening I feel sick to my stomach. I panic for a moment and try desperately not to hyperventilate at the situation. I can't do it again. I look out the ambulance window and consider asking my colleague to pull over so I make a run for it, but I resist.

Somehow, despite my mind screaming, shouting, swearing to stop, to turn around never to return, my legs keep moving forwards in an autonomic motion towards the scene, as I exit the cab. I am unruffled on the surface, a professional. I guess that's why my new ECA today looks at me funny when I don't laugh at one if his joke's I normally find hysterical.

As we enter the scene, I'm hit with so much relief and joy when I see and hear the sights and sounds of a pink, screaming, healthy, perfect new born baby, I could cry. But I don't. I missed the birth, but I don't care one bit. In fact, on this occasion I'm pleased I did miss it, because the scene I walked into was just so perfect, I wouldn't change anything about it for a single thing on this earth. Besides, the Mum of now five seems to have coped remarkably well all by herself! I'm in awe of her.

Just as I compose myself -again(!)- this time out of shire elation, the midwife pulls up and apologises repetitively for the delay.

There's really no requirement for us to remain on scene once we've performed a full patient and baby assessment, placenta is delivered and the midwife is happy for both parties to remain on scene, but I just can't bear to put the neonate* down, who I've just been handed. So we stay a further thirty minutes to take in the unique, heart-warming moment.

When we do finally arrive back at station, beaming with joy and satisfaction, skipping into the crew room, I'm called in to my managers office.

"Can I have a word a minute Georgia?" she asks quietly, whilst I put a pot of coffee on, away from the rest of the staff.

'What on earth have I done wrong now?' I think to myself. 'I've only just come back to work!'

"I heard about the maternity job you had. It can be hard getting a job like that on your first couple of shifts back. I just wanted to check you're ready to return to work after that call out?"

I pause for a second as I think about my options, but in actual fact I have already decided within a matter of a second. I love what I do, and I never want to give it up.

"I'm ready" I reply confidently, really meaning that.

Glossary (in order of sequence):

NOF*- Neck of femur/hip fracture.

Subarachnoid brain haemorrhage*- A burst blood vessel, causing blood to pool in the space between the brain and the skull.

RRV*- Rapid Response Vehicle.

Endotracheal (ET) tube *- a measured to fit plastic tube is inserted into the unconscious patient's trachea to maintain their airway, and facilitate adequate oxygenation. In hospital, ET tubes are often used to manage a patient's airway during anaesthetic. But on the ambulance, paramedics' only insert ET tubes into deceased patients, as road paramedics cannot anaesthetise.

Flashback*- blood exiting the opposite end of the cannula, which confirms correct placement.
Rhythm check*- every two minutes during a resuscitation attempt, chest compressions are withheld for a matter of seconds whilst the patient's heart rhythm is established.

Intraosseous (IO)*- Injecting a catheter directly into the bone of the tibia (shin bone) or the humeral head (upper arm) to administer drugs when cannulation is unsuccessful or unavailable.

Category one (cat one)*- Categories range from 'cat one' to 'cat five' with one being the highest priority call out, where it is a matter of life and death. And five is the least priority job.

Primary Percutaneous Coronary Intervention (PPCI)* - where patients having a heart attack are taken straight into the coronary care unit to have a stent fitted via a catheter, opening up the affected occluded artery. Previously known as angioplasty.

ST segment elevation myocardial infarction (STEMI)* - A myocardial infarction is a heart attack, a ST elevation segment myocardial infarction simply means the heart attack is severe enough to cause abnormal changes to the ST segment on an ECG.

Absence attack* - a type of seizure most common in children, causing a patient to black out or stare into space for a few seconds.

Electroencephalography (EEG)* - monitors and records the electrical activity in the brain.

Electrocardiogram (ECG)*- measures the cardiac rhythm, identifying any electrical changes in each heartbeat.

Oxygen saturations*- a pulse oximeter measures the percentage of oxygen in the bloodstream.
Chronic obstructive pulmonary disease (COPD)*- a chronic inflammation lung disease.

Hypertensive*- high blood pressure.

Tachycardia*- an abnormally fast heart rate.

National early warning score (NEWS2)* - a sepsis screening tool determining the severity of the patient's condition based on their current vital signs, from zero to twenty. Zero being medically fit, and anything over five or six (depending on which textbook you read) being a medical emergency requiring immediate treatment.

Transient ischemic attack (TIA)* - a temporary occlusion to one of the brain's blood vessels causing stroke symptoms for twenty four hours or less, usually with a full recovery. Also called a 'mini stroke'.

Hemiplegic migraine*- a rare migraine which presents itself with stroke symptoms.

Bell's palsy*- An infection that causes temporary weakness to the facial nerve on one side of the face, causing unilateral (one sided) facial droop, mimicking a stroke.

Time is brain*- A term often used in regard to strokes, since healthy nervous tissue is lost rapidly during a stroke.

Pre alert/ATMIST*- (Age, Time, Mechanism of injury, Injuries, Signs and symptoms, Treatment) A heads up to the receiving hospital on the severity of the patient's condition.

Haemorrhagic stroke*- A stroke caused by a burst blood vessel as opposed to an occluded blood vessel (a clot).

Hypoxia*- Dangerously low level of oxygen in the blood stream.

Nebuliser*- a special oxygen mask filled with medicines which help you breath when your airways are constricted.

Auscultate/auscultation*- listening with a stethoscope.

Acidotic/acidosis*- Too much acid in the body fluids, occurring when the lungs and kidneys can no longer keep your pH in balance. Most of the bodies processes produce acid. Bronchodilation* is the widening of the lower airways, allowing air to move freely in and out of the lungs.

Hematemesis*- vomiting blood.

Hypovolemic shock*- a reduced volume of circulating blood in the body causing multi organ failure.

Tranexamic acid (TXA)*- a drug which treats or prevents excessive blood loss.

DOA*- Dead on arrival.

Carotid pulse*- a pulse point at the neck.

Hypertension*- high blood pressure.

Appendectomy*- Surgical removal of the appendix.

HEMS (helicopter emergency medical service)*- Air medical service providing enhanced care and fast transportation to appropriate hospitals.

Analgesia*- pain relief.

Entonox*- gas and air/ nitrous oxide.

Antiemetic*- anti-sickness.

Scapula*- shoulder blade.

Arteriole*- Arterioles connect the arteries to the capillaries.

Baryatric*- Overweight or obese.

Hypovolaemic shock*- When the body loses approximately 20% of its blood volume at a minimum, meaning the heart cannot pump enough blood around the body, no matter how fast it beats, or how constricted the blood vessels become.

Surgical emphysema*- Air that has escaped from a lacerated lung, causing air pockets where they shouldn't be. Often a result of a pneumothorax.

Pneumothorax*- a collapsed lung causing air to spread in the space between the lung and the chest wall. In a tension pneumothorax, the air can be expired from the punctured sight but not inspired, so with every breath the lung becomes crushed.

Cardiogenic shock*- The heart suddenly cannot pump enough blood around the body to meet the body's demands, which is fatal if not treated quickly. This is often as a result of a defect to the heart itself, as opposed to a lack of circulating volume.

Supraventricular tachycardia (SVT)*- the cardiac cells where the heartbeat originates are excitable, creating an abnormally fast heart rate, which cannot be maintained for long periods of time.

GCS (Glasgow Coma Scale)* - A neurological scoring system from three to fifteen. Three is completely unresponsive, whilst fifteen is lucid and comatose.

Functional neurological disorder (FND)* - The name given to a set of neurological symptoms caused by faulty neurological pathways, that doesn't originate from a physical disease or disorder. It is thought the cause is both neurological and mental illness combined.

However, the most recent data argues that the FND is a result of defective white/brain matter.

Tonic clonic seizure* - Previously known as a grand mal seizure, a tonic clonic seizure is what most people think of when they hear the word convulsion, or fit. The patient becomes rigid before all their limbs thrash uncontrollably. The patient is not conscious during a tonic clonic seizure.

Electrolyte imbalance* - An abnormality in the concentration of electrolytes (sodium, potassium etc.) in the human body.

Postictal phase* - Confusion, drowsiness and an altered level of consciousness immediately following a seizure, usually a tonic clonic seizure. It is a completely normal reaction whilst the brain resets itself.

STEMI with right ventricular involvement* - An inferior heart attack affecting the right side of the heart muscle, which facilitates the pulmonary circuit. The pulmonary system perfuses the lungs, providing them with oxygen rich blood, so an occlusion on the right side of the heart can cause compromised respiration.

Heart failure* - With age or progressive cardiac disease, the left side of the heart becomes weaker, meaning less blood is pumped out of its ventricle and forced around the body. This causes a build-up of stagnant blood backing up in the left atrium, the pulmonary vein and the lungs, which causes pulmonary oedema (fluid on the lungs, where if severe and acute enough, the lungs will eventually drown in their own fluid- however this is more than often a chronic lengthy process. Acute is only common in altitude sickness and trauma). This is called left ventricular (heart) failure. Progressively, the heart becomes even weaker and blood continues backing up until it stagnates in the systemic circulation (whole body), particularly pooling in the ankles. This is then congestive heart failure, AKA right ventricular failure.

Unstable angina* - narrowing of the coronary arteries at rest, as a result of cholesterol build up.

Syncope*- a faint.

Vasodilation*- widening of the blood vessels.

Hypotension*- Low blood pressure.

Priority one backup* - like a cat 1 call out, but requested by another clinician already on scene. A patient who is either in cardiac arrest, seizing, or presents an immediate threat to life.

Haematoma* - a collection of blood pooling outside of blood vessels. AKA, in this case, a large lump on the head.

Horizontal gaze* - fixed gaze to the left or the right, dependant on which side of the brain is impaired, often as a result of an acute cerebral vascular event, including but not limited to a stroke.

Bradycardia* - Slow heart rate.

Aspiration* - breathing in foreign objects.

Sub-dural haemorrhage* - A brain haemorrhage within the sub-dural space (one of the three layers between the skull and the brain). The blood pools within the sub-dural space causing a haematoma, which compresses the brain if not removed.

Rigors*- severe shivers caused by a high temperature.

Costochondritis* - Inflammation of the intercostals muscles causing a sharp pain around the ribs and sternum (breastbone), which is worsened by movement and inspiration.

Clopidogrel* - an antiplatelet medication/ blood thinner.

Septic shock* - A systemic abnormal response to an infection causing multi organ injury.

Hypoglycaemia* - Low blood sugars, most commonly associated with diabetes.

F1 doctor* - Foundation one doctor. Their first year out of medical school as a junior doctor.

Post ROSC (Return of Spontaneous Circulation) care*- An attempt to maintain ROSC and prevent the patient from re-arresting.

Abdominal aortic aneurysm (triple A)*- An aneurysm (a bulge in a blood vessel which may eventually burst, depending on its size and other contributing factors) in the largest artery in the human body.

Rapid sequence intubation (RSI)*- Anesthetising the patient before intubating them.

Amitriptyline* - an antidepressant, as well as a medication sometimes used to treat pain and migraines.

Pyrexia* - a fever.

Hyper-extended chest* - Over inflation of the lungs, where air becomes trapped in the small airways. Most common in COPD (Chronic Obstructive Pulmonary Disease) and
asthma.

Agonal breathing* - gasping for breath pre -or during- respiratory and/or cardiac arrest. Agonal breathing is not a true form of breathing compatible with life. It is simply a reflex created by the brainstem.

ROSC* - Return of spontaneous circulation.

Primary survey* - A quick, effective and structured way of determining the severity of the patient, using a CABCDE approach (Catastrophic haemorrhage, Airway, Breathing, Circulation, Disability, Evaluation). Originally derived from the military.

16 gauge cannula*- Second from largest cannula we carry. The gauge is the width of the needle.

Long bones*- The femurs (thigh bones) and humorous bones (Upper arm bones). The Tibia, Fibula (lower leg bones), Ulna and Radius (Lower arm bones) are also sometimes classified as long
bones.

FLAPS TWELVE*- Part of the B (breathing) assessment on the primary survey. The acronym FLAPS stands for: Feel, Look, Auscultate, Percuss and Search (the chest for injuries), whilst TWELVE stands for: Tracheal deviation (deviation of the windpipe to the left or right, usually due a punctured lung- tension pneumothorax), Wounds (primarily to the chest or airways), surgical Emphysema (air bubbles trapped in the chest cavity), Laryngeal injury, Venous distension (JVP- Jugular venous distension), and Expose/Evaluate.

Furosemide* - a diuretic (water tablet). It decreases the amount of anti-diuretic hormone (ADH) released into the body.

Central vertigo* - a spinning sensation whilst remaining still, causing stationary objects to appear is if they are moving, as a result of a deficit to the central nervous system (CNS).This differs from peripheral vertigo, which presents with similar initial symptoms, but originates from the inner ear, and is much less time critical.

Bilateral nystagmus* - a visual disturbance in which both of the eye balls quiver (make small repetitive uncontrolled movements) from side to side. Often, if acute, nystagmus occurs unilaterally (one sided), as a result of an inner ear infection, pointing in the direction of the infected ear. But, if it occurs acutely and bilaterally (both sides), it is usually a result of a neurological event, such as a stroke.

Pulse pressure* - The difference between the systolic (top number) and the diastolic (bottom number). The greater the difference in numbers, the wider the pulse pressure (E.g. 120/80- normal pulse pressure. 190/60- widened pulse pressure).

Cushing's Triad*- Widened pulse pressure, bradycardia and a slow respiratory rate, in that order, which suggests raising intra-cranial pressure.

Intra-cranial Pressure (ICP)* - swelling of the brain tissue itself, or the tissues surrounding the brain, usually caused by lesions or blood. As ICP rises, the brain becomes crushed. Eventually the medulla oblongata (the brains respiratory centre) will be crushed, causing abnormal breathing and respiratory arrest.

Anticonvulsants* - used for the treatment of seizures.

Beta blockers* - they slow the heart rate, by inhibiting the chemical epinephrine, which in turn lowers blood pressure.

Angiotensin converting enzyme (ACE) inhibitors* - they dilate (relax) the blood vessels and decrease blood volume, lowering blood pressure.

Osmotic diuretics* - a diuretic drug (water tablet) which inhibits the re-absorption of sodium and water.

90/55* (Blood pressure interpretation)- 120/80 is an ideal blood pressure. Anything below 90 (the first/top number) is classed as hypotensive (low blood pressure).

Hypovolemia* - blood volume depletion (blood loss, usually as a result of trauma) or severe body fluid loss (burns, severe continuous diarrhoea and vomiting). In hypovalaemic shock, the body has lost enough extracellular fluid, or blood, to cause a dangerously low blood pressure, hypothermia (as our blood retains all of our heat) and potentially fatality.

Epipen* - a medical device carried by anaphylactic patients, to self administer a measured dose of adrenaline when required.

Stridor* - a high pitched wheezy sound originating in the upper airway, as a result on an obstruction or severe inflammation.

Hypotension* - Low blood pressure.

Histamine* - Histamine plays an important part in the human body's immune response. It is released in response to an allergen. An allergen could be pollen, or the body's abnormal response to an everyday item (insect bite, latex, nuts, balloons etc). It's intention is to help the body fight off the unwanted allergen by producing local inflammation and a hives rash. However, in anaphylaxis too much histamine is released. This causes systemic (multi-organ) inflammation. if left untreated, this will cause anaphylactic shock and death. Anti-histamines inhibit the histamine response, preventing the symptoms from deteriorating further.

Tripod position * - where a patient sits or leans forward with their hands on their knees gasping for breath. This position enables maximum possible air entry.

Deltoid muscle* - the muscle in the upper arm and uppermost shoulder.

Cyanotic*- Blue, due to a lack of oxygen.

Bagging a patient*- Using a bag-valve mask over the patients' nose and mouth to provide them with oxygen when they are not breathing - or breathing effectively - for themselves.

Thrombolysis* - a powerful drug which rapidly dissolves a blood clot, however these drugs have potentially fatal complications. For this reason, and with PPCI becoming so readily available nowadays, thrombolytic drugs are no longer carried by road paramedics in urban areas such as mine.

Opioid* - a strong narcotic medication used for pain relief (e.g. morphine), or illegally as heroin.

Distal ulna and distal radius* - the part of the forearm bones which connect to the wrist.

Profolol* - a drug which decreases a patients level of consciousness. Administered by an anaesthetist who titrates the dose according to how long they wish to keep their patient unconscious.

Anaesthetists cubicle* - A small room where you are put to sleep before they wheel you through the double doors into the operating theatre.

Datix*- An incident management system.

FFP3 masks*- A disposable filtering facepiece mask made from synthetic fibre, to provide respiratory protection.

Immunocompromised*- The immune systems defences are low.

Aerosol generating procedures (AGPs)*- Any medical procedure which stimulate the release of air born particles.

Tyvek suit*- A coverall, protecting its users from aerosols, micro-organisms, hazardous and non-hazardous dry particles and liquid splash.

Basic Life Support (BLS)*- A series of non-invasive medical procedures and protocols performed during a cardiac arrest until ALS can be provided by a higher trained clinician. BLS primarily comprises of chest compressions, oxygenation and defibrillation in an attempt to restart a patient's heart.

Advanced Life Support (ALS)*- A series of invasive and non-invasive procedures and protocols as well as drug therapy, which extends beyond BLS, used on patients in cardiac arrest, in an attempt to restart their heart.

Bradypnea*- Slow respiration rate.

Narcan*- Naloxone, most commonly called by its brand name: Narcan, is a drug used to reverse the effects of opioids (morphine, fentanyl heroine, to name a few).

Narcotics*- Opioids.

Apnoeic*- A cessation of breathing.

Track marks*- Discolouration and scaring running along veins, which have been damaged from frequent intravenous (IV) drug use.

Perineum*- The anatomy between the anus and genitals.

Thoracotomy*- A procedure where an emergency surgical incision is made between the ribs to allow medics access to the thoracic cavity to perform invasive intervention during a traumatic cardiac arrest.

Peritoneum*- A membranous lining covering the abdominal organs.

Gestation period*- Weeks pregnant.

Endometrial tissue*- The tissue that lines the uterus.

Neonate*- A new born baby.

Acknowledgements

The author would like to thank Andrew Combes for his continued support, and Christoph Schroth, Shirley Rutherford and Alex James, without whom, this book would not have been possible.

Printed in Great Britain
by Amazon